THE WHITE PEAK WAY

The Manifold Valley from Thor's Cave

THE WHITE PEAK WAY

A 90-Mile Circular Walk in the
Peak National Park

by

ROBERT HASLAM

CICERONE PRESS,
MILNTHORPE, CUMBRIA

© Robert Haslam 1982, 1990
First published 1982
Reprinted 1985
New Edition 1990
Revised reprint 1997
ISBN 1 85284 056 0

Sketch maps and drawings by Ann Dobell.
Photographs by Dave Barnett.
Water colour paintings by my late Father, Ron Haslam.

CONTENTS

The White Peak Way

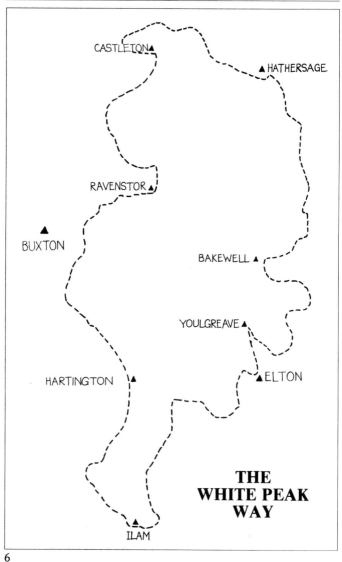

THE
WHITE PEAK
WAY

PREFACE

The best thing that can be said for long distance paths supported by national agencies or local government is that they are well maintained. On the other side of the coin it could be argued that many suffer from over-zealous waymarking. I am of the school which believes map, compass and guidebook should suffice, and that plotting and following your chosen route should be an integral part of the walk. I feel something of the spirit of the journey is lost when every footstep is already highlighted on your map and emblazoned on every tree, stile and gate.

Don't get me wrong, I am not totally against waymarking. In woodland and on commons, where numerous paths intersect, it is a blessing, as long as it is discrete.

Specific waymarking also imposes limits on planning. The tendency is to stick to the yellow brick road, thus limiting your options with regard to daily mileage and availability of accommodation. Free from such restrictions, an unwaymarked route is more easily adjusted to best suit individual needs.

Since its inception in 1982, the White Peak Way has escaped official adoption, nevertheless it has evolved into one of the most popular unofficial recreational walking routes in Britain.

The level of path maintenance is high as the route lies wholly within the Peak National Park, who do an excellent job renewing stiles, gates and signs.

And when it comes to planning, the WPW is more flexible than most. Being circular it can be joined wherever you wish, and walked in whichever direction you choose, both clockwise and anti-clockwise directions are given. It is also the only long distance path that offers a choice of youth hostel, campsite or bed and breakfast at the end of every stage. And with so much accommodation now available on and close to the route, planning your schedule has never been easier. A new feature is the Information Table in Appendix IV, which shows at a glance where accommodation and other facilities can be found.

As with the earlier editions, this guide contains detailed notes on equipment and preparation, planning and accommodation, maps, viewpoints, and the ever-popular pub guide.

At the end of the day though, what matters most is the scenic quality of the route. The White Peak Way encompasses some of the most varied, spectacular and beautiful countryside in England. That alone is the main reason for its continuing popularity.

INTRODUCTION

The Peak District is noted for magnificent scenery and fresh air, despite being an island surrounded by a sea of industrial conurbations. Contained within the bounds of the Peak District National Park is a wealth of natural beauty and as diverse a landscape as is found anywhere in Britain.

The contrast is due to the dissimilarity of the underlying rock types. The far north of the region is Millstone Grit, covered with a thick mantle of peat, riven in places with deep tortuous channels - the infamous groughs of Kinder, Bleaklow and Black Hill, the bane of every Pennine Wayfarer. This tableland of bleak heather moor stands in splendid isolation at around 2,000 feet at the southern end of the Pennines.

Towards the centre a weaker, finer-grained gritstone prevails, one which is easily eroded, incising the moors with deep valleys such as the Vale of Edale and the Upper Derwent. At higher elevations boggy cotton grass is more prevalent than heather and is, in the absence of acidic peat, intermingled with bracken, bilberry and gorse. The gritstone moors are water-gathering and the vales ideal catchment basins, so many contain reservoirs. Some, like Longdendale, are an eyesore; but others, like in the Upper Derwent Valley, have been enhanced by the planting of trees and good management.

This half of the park is the so-called Dark Peak, where ramblers enjoy unrestricted access (except during the grouse shooting season). However it is no place for the ill-equiped and inexperienced. The harsh, featureless terrain and unpredictable weather mean that expertise with map and compass is essential.

Further south the gritstone has been worn away to reveal a central dome of Carboniferous Limestone, flanked down the east and west by narrow bands of grit. The distinctive characteristic of these flanks are north to south running escarpments of Millstone Grit called 'edges'. These are especially well pronounced on the eastern side overlooking the Derwent Valley. Their well trodden crests provide walkers with superlative views throughout their entire length.

The pastoral limestone plateau stands between 1,000 and 1,500 feet and is fairly level and open, bearing few trees except for isolated coppices of ash grouped around upland farmsteads. Charming stone-built villages are dotted about the plateau, usually at points where spring water emerges. The larger settlements, which are equally attractive and unspoilt, are congregated along the lines of communication in the broader river valleys on the periphery.

The limey soil is too thin and poor for arable farming or forestry so livestock farming predominates. The verdant pasture supports a rich and varied flora, and is divided into fields by an immense chequerboard of light-grey drystone walls - the symbolic feature of the White Peak.

The principal and most spectacular feature of limestone country is the dales. Without rivers they are shallow, with rounded scree-littered slopes below rocky crests. Some may have only semi-permanent streams, like Lathkill Dale and the Manifold Valley. These are deeper and more densely wooded, with larger outcroppings of rock. Most impressive of all are the few dales that do contain rivers, like Dovedale and the Wye Dales. These appear as deep narrow gorges with sheer, rocky sides and thickly wooded bottoms from which emanate spires, tors and pinnacles, weathered into the most fantastic shapes.

The White Peak Way, during the course of its meandering 90-mile circuit, explores the hills and dales of limestone country and the gritstone moors and edges to the east. It also visits many of the area's most notable landmarks, places of interest and sites of antiquity. The journey is divided into seven comfortable stages, each linked by a youth hostel, although campsites and bed and breakfast accommodation are always close by. The variety and grandeur of scenery guarantees an interesting and memorable holiday for the discerning rambler.

MAPS

The whole of the route can be followed on the 1-inch Tourist Map of the Peak District, or on OS Landranger Sheets 110 and 119. The best maps for walkers are the detailed 1:25,000 Outdoor Leisure series - The White Peak and The Dark Peak.

EQUIPMENT AND PREPARATION

Because it only takes a week, and is divided into comfortable stages, many walkers choose the White Peak Way as their first long distance walk, or as an introduction to children of the delights of the trail. In my experience of leading walks, many newcomers seem to adopt the policy of getting from A to B as quickly as possible, then spending the rest of the afternoon strolling or relaxing without the burden of a heavy pack. On the face of it this seems like a sound idea, however it is the increased friction inside your boots induced by walking fast that causes blisters. You will cause much less damage by pacing yourself over the eight hours or so available. Stop for five minutes every hour for a pack-break, like the army do, or remove your pack every time you stop for a slurp or to take a photo. Relieving that pressure from your shoulders, if only for a few minutes, has an invigorating effect. Try and take at least two long breaks of about half an hour during the day, time permitting, whether that involves sitting in the pub, sprawled out in the sun or sheltering from the rain. Believe me, there's nothing worse than pain for marring the enjoyment of a walking holiday.

It would be folly to attempt a long distance walk without adequate preparation. New boots need to be worn in, feet hardened, muscles strengthened and equipment chosen, sorted and finally packed so that the load lies comfortably on your back yet weighs as little as possible - for weight is the walker's enemy and every effort should be made to restrict the load to essentials.

By staying in hostels or guest houses you eliminate the bulk of tent, sleeping bag and cooking gear, which basically only leaves clothes and food. Only two sets of clothing are necessary - one to wear during the day and a change for evening (let others worry about the smell!). A pair of shorts and a T-shirt are ideal in summer, supplemented with a woollen pullover in case it grows cool. A shirt, jeans, spare under-wear and trainers will suffice for evening. You will, of course, need a set of waterproofs, and I would advise you bring a woollen hat, gloves and a spare sweater. It can grow mighty cool on the hills, even in summer.

Buy food on a daily basis - it is very unlikely you will be lost in the wilds of Derbyshire for days on end with only raw sheep to live off, so it is pointless carrying more than you need. For hot drinks you will obviously need a thermos flask; however, I would not fill it with tea or coffee as these tend to stew very quickly when on the move, necessitating the use of a spoon. Fill it with boiling water instead (sweetened if wanted) and carry tea bags, coffee and powdered milk.

All the little odds and ends like soap, toothbrush, toothpaste, comb, plasters, aspirin, moleskin (good for blisters), safety pin, tissues, knife etc. can be carried in a toilet bag. Add to this a towel, the relevant maps, guidebook and money and you have the essentials. Binoculars, camera, nightwear, reading material and portable toilet must all be considered luxuries and only taken if you are confident of handling the extra weight. However, do take a spare set of walking socks in case you get an accidental soaking (there are a couple of sets of stepping stones to negotiate!).

Start your build-up about a month before the holiday by walking both days every weekend, carrying a full pack so that your body grows accustomed to the weight. Don't be a chicken and be put off by the rain. You may as well become used to it beforehand since with our climate it is almost certain to rain sometime during the week. Anyway, once you are thoroughly soaked walking in the rain can be quite exhilarating, especially in woodland. The pounding of raindrops on the leafy canopy, the sheen of wet vegetation and the dim light coalesce in a magical spell of sight and sound. While you remain on the move you will be warm and comfortable despite the wet - until it starts to dribble down your neck, that is.

PLANNING AND ACCOMMODATION

The White Peak Way is the only long distance path in Britain which offers walkers the choice of a campsite, youth hostel or bed and breakfast accommodation at the end of every stage. The main route is measured and described from hostel to hostel, although no major diversions are needed to locate campsites, camping barns or B&B. In high summer and during Bank Holidays it would be advisable to book in advance.

Bakewell, Youlgreave, Ilam Hall, Hartington, Ravenstor, Castleton and Hathersage are the designated youth hostels, although Elton and Buxton are also convenient. YHA operate a Booking Bureau for the WPW so that members may book all their accommodation inclusive. For details send a SAE to White Peak Way Booking Bureau, YHA Northern Region, PO Box 11, Matlock, Derbyshire, DE4 2XA. Tel: 01426 939215 (calls at local rate 24hrs).

Whether you use this service or not, remember to consult the current YHA handbook with regard to closed nights. Further hostel information is given in Appendix II.

There a number of campsites and camping barns lying close to the Way. The camping barns at Bakewell, Birchover, Middleton, Losehill, Edale and Upper Booth are run by the National Park and must be booked in advance. Contact the Peak National Park Office, Aldern House, Baslow Road, Bakewell, DE5 1AE. Tel: 01629 816316. Camping barn leaflets are available from Tourist Information Centres.

The campsites are touring caravan sites in the main which offer pitches for tents. They are marked on OS maps and are best contacted through the Caravan and Camping leaflet published annually by the National Park and available from Tourist Information Centres.

As the White Peak Way has grown in popularity, the number of establishments offering accommodation on and close to the route has increased markedly. This includes hotels, pubs, farms and guest houses, in isolated spots as well as in villages. Listings of names and addresses would not therefore provide a true reflection of what is currently available. I therefore advise you to contact the Tourist Information Office in Bakewell and request the current Derbyshire Dales and Peak National Park Accommodation Guides, both of which are free.

Bakewell Tourist Information Centre,
Old Market Hall,
Bridge Street,
Bakewell,
DE4 1DS
Tel: 01629 813227

The Derbyshire section of the current Ramblers' Handbook and

13

Accommodation Guide is another good source, with numerous bed and breakfast listings under the White Peak Way heading.

To help plan your itinerary turn to the Information Table in Appendix IV, which shows at a glance where on the route all the above can be found.

BAKEWELL

In 1951 the Peak District became the first area in Britain to be designated as a National Park. The Peak Park Joint Planning Board, which administers the park, has its headquarters at Bakewell, the only town within the park boundary and therefore rightly known as the capital of the Peak

Surrounded by wooded hills in the broadest part of the Wye Valley, Bakewell is a predominantly stone-built market town trading principally in livestock. Its central location and accessibility are the main reasons for choosing Bakewell as the focus for the walk. There are nearby mainline railway stations at Sheffield, Chesterfield and Derby. Regular bus services operate from these centres as well as from Matlock, Nottingham and Manchester, via Buxton.

If you intend spending the first night at Bakewell, prior to beginning the walk, you should have ample time for exploration. The best place to start is the National Park Information Centre in Bridge Street. The building dates from the seventeenth century and was originally the market hall. The numerous leaflets and artistic visual displays provide a valuable insight into the countryside through which you are about to travel.

A detailed insight into Bakewell's own history can be gained by visiting the Old House Museum (signposted from the roundabout and open daily from Easter to the end of September from 2.30pm to 5.00pm). Built in the fifteenth century as a parsonage, the building was purchased by Sir Richard Arkwright in 1796 to house workers for his cotton spinning mill (now demolished). When the mill closed in 1860 the house was sold, and it then passed through various hands until 1955 when the Bakewell Historical Society converted it into a local history museum.

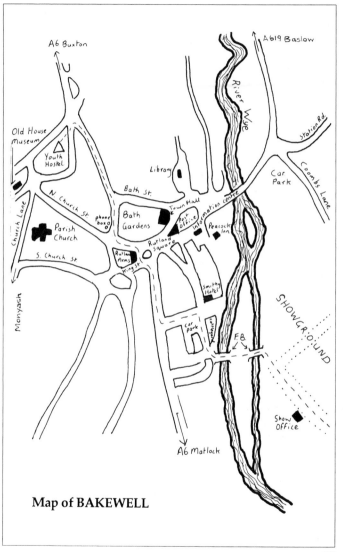

Map of BAKEWELL

Information Centre, Bakewell

The well preserved shaft of a Saxon cross stands in the graveyard of the parish church, and a number of carved stones from the same period are to be found in the porch and interior. The south transept houses elaborate monuments to members of the Vernon family, the landed gentry who resided at nearby Haddon Hall from the twelfth to the sixteenth century. Also of interest is the font which was carved in the fourteenth century from a single block of gritstone; the finest of its kind in Derbyshire.

Fronting the colourful Bath Gardens, which face onto Rutland Square, is the Bath House. Built for the Duke of Rutland in 1697 it contains a huge bath, 33ft long by 16ft wide, which is fed by warm springs. Bakewell is actually a spa, but historians have kept this a secret, probably because no one ever got cured! This could be the reason the Bath House is not open to the public. The Old Town Hall and Courthouse on King Street is not open either, though a notice in the window tells of its history.

Jane Austen stayed at the Rutland Arms in 1811 and mentions it in *Pride and Prejudice*, referring to Bakewell as Lambton. The famous

Bakewell Bridge

Bakewell Tart - or Pudding as it is known locally, for obvious reasons - was first baked at the hotel by accident when a cook misread instructions for making a strawberry jam tart and poured the egg mixture over the jam instead of using it to make the pastry. The Pudding Shop in Bridge Street sells puddings made to the original recipe, though not baked by the same cook!

There are also pleasant riverside walks both up and downstream from the five-arched road bridge, originally founded on this site in about 1300. Given time you might also consider visiting Haddon Hall, which is situated about 2 miles down the A6 towards Matlock. Follow the riverbank footpath.

VIEWPOINTS

When walking over unfamiliar territory it is difficult to know in advance the best stopping places for meal breaks and rests. You may find a cosy nook in which to eat your sarnies, then no sooner having set off again you discover a spot twice as good. This is very irritating, and to help overcome it I have indicated suitable stopping places by inserting the word 'viewpoint' in brackets at the appropriate point in the text. These are either sites of special interest (excluding pubs) or vantage points with wide ranging views.

BADGES

White Peak Way sew-on badges are available from: P & R Publicity Ltd., Queensway, Stem Lane Industrial Estate, New Milton, Hampshire, BU25 5NN. Tel: 01425 611911.

ROUTE MAP KEY

Scale: Approx. 1¼ inches to a mile
North is top of the map

- - - - White Peak Way   · — · — · — Other footpaths

━━━━ Motor road   ⋯⋯⋯⋯⋯ Unenclosed road
                                                          or farm track

+━+━+━+ Railway

                                              +•+•+•+•+ Disused railway

ᴏᴏᴏᴏᴏᴏ Wall   ᴏ ᴏ ᴏ ᴏ Broken wall

+++++++ Fence   ı ı ı ı ı ı Broken fence

∼∼∼➞ Stream or river – arrow indicates direction of flow

SYMBOLS

⟁⟁ᗛᗛ Trees   🏠 Buildings   ⟋⟍⟋⟍ Rocks
  △ Youth hostel   ✚ Church   ✗ Campsite
  ⇞ Viewpoint   )[Bridge   ᴏ Place of interest

ABBREVIATIONS

SP Signpost   Q   Quarry
FB Footbridge   PH Public House

The plan of Bakewell and other villages are not drawn to scale

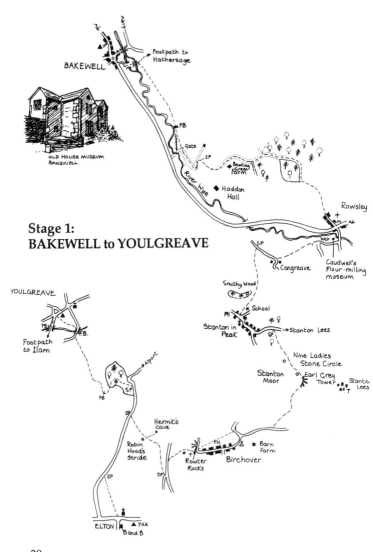

Stage 1:
BAKEWELL to YOULGREAVE

THE WHITE PEAK WAY

Stage 1: Bakewell to Youlgreave   12 miles

(Alternative: Bakewell to Elton 10 miles.)

You will see from the map opposite that it is but a short step from Bakewell to Youlgreave as the crow flies. Your route may be circuitous, yet it covers a variety of terrain and has something of interest round every bend. Kids of all ages will love it. There are rocks to scramble on, a hidden cave, a prehistoric stone circle, a working flour mill and one of the finest houses in England. You pass through two contrasting villages, one in an idyllic valley setting, the other an estate village clinging to a hillside. And there is a pub halfway noted for its lunchtime meals. Altogether a fascinating and rewarding ramble over the environs of Stanton Moor.

Bakewell has all the amenities a walker needs, plus there is a tea shop in Rowsley, and pubs in Rowsley, Stanton and Birchover. Youlgreave has pubs, B&B, a youth hostel and a chip shop. Elton has a tea room, youth hostel, B&B and pub.

Descend steeply from the youth hostel and turn right along the A6, continuing beyond the roundabout to take the first road on the left. Turn right opposite the hotel and walk past the livestock market to the river, crossing two footbridges to enter the showground. This is the site of the annual Bakewell Show, one of the largest, most important and well patronised agricultural shows in the country. The pretty route is along the riverside promenade from the road bridge, but be warned - if you are carrying food you will almost certainly be mugged by ducks!

Carry on down the road past the Agricultural Society office. When it bends to the left continue ahead on the same line across fields, as directed by the yellow arrow on the gate. You will see plenty of these helpful waymarking symbols today, and indeed throughout the

Peacock Hotel, Rowsley

week. They are sometimes numbered to indicate a particular route and are commonplace in the Peak. Although helpful as a direction indicator, one should not suppose them to be peculiar to The White Peak Way, which is not waymarked. Life is never easy!

You are soon joined by the river, on which you are likely to see moorhen, coot and mallard. A short while later the path climbs away from the bank to follow a fence to a gate. Turn left up the track, climbing steadily through the trees until, after a hairpin bend, a gate on the right admits to fields. Stay close to the railings through three gates to join the track passing Bowling Green Farm. There is a good chance of surprising pheasant and partridge which fly off with a startled cry and a loud beating of wings, thus inducing heart failure.

Bear left when the track reaches a Y-junction, then at the next fork turn right past the metal barrier. This path is followed down through the wood into the village of Rowsley, ignoring all paths joining from the left. The main road is met beside the Peacock Hotel, an Elizabethan-style manor house built in 1652. It took them until 1828 to turn it into a pub. The hotel took its name from the stone peacock above the entrance which is part of the Manners' coat of arms.

Cross the A6 and follow the Stanton-in-Peak road, which turns sharp right to run between the river and the cricket ground. Caudwell's Mill, which is beyond the car park just before the bridge, is a worthwhile diversion. There is plenty to see and refreshments are available.

Leave the road at the next bend and continue beside the Wye. Almost immediately the path begins to climb, rounding the side of the hill following a bend in the river. An old stone gatepost between two trees then gives you the line, and for a short distance you walk alongside the dyke on your left before bearing right across the field to the wood in the far corner. Descend through the trees then skirt the hill to gain the road at Cóngreave via a stile next to a gate.

Turn right down the hill, taking to the fields again at the Stanton in Peak footpath sign. Bear half-left to a footbridge concealed in the hedge near the field corner then ascend the next field, passing to the right of the solitary tree to a squeezer beneath the large sweet chestnut ahead. Continue diagonally up the hill through a series of gateways and stiles. Beyond a stone cattle byre you continue on a plainer line alongside a wood, guided in the latter stages by the steeple of Stanton church. You join a lane which passes the school to emerge on the road opposite the war memorial.

There are superb retrospective views back down the Wye Valley to Bakewell on this climb. Note the impressive sight of Haddon Hall nestling amidst the trees in the foreground. Most of the building was undertaken by the Vernons, who occupied the hall from 1170 to 1567. In 1558 Dorothy, the daughter and heiress of Sir George Vernon, eloped with John Manners, the second son of the first Earl of Rutland. They married, and upon the death of Sir George in 1567 took possession, the hall thus becoming part of the Manners' estates. There followed a further spate of building and alteration but this ceased abruptly in the seventeenth century when the earl moved to the Manners' other seat at Belvoir Castle in Leicestershire. The Dukes of Rutland have resided there ever since.

Architecturally, this loss of favour was the best thing that could have happened to Haddon, for it remained neglected for the next two hundred years. The tenth duke decided it was ready for a clean and had the place restored to its former glory at the beginning of this

23

Earl Grey Tower, Stanton Moor

century, since when it has become one of the best loved houses in England, attracting thousands of visitors every year.

As you climb the hill through the village look out for the interwoven initials WT carved on the door lintels of some of the houses. These were built by William Thornhill, who lived at nearby Stanton Hall. It was probably the first housing estate in Britain.

Walk up the minor road signposted 'Stanton Lees $1^1/2$' and at the top of the hill turn right along the track leading across fields to Stanton Moor - a prominent outlying mass of gritstone rising to over 1,000 feet above sea-level. This small island of open heather moor is

24

a delight to explore, riddled as it is with ancient burial mounds and old quarry workings. It would take a week to discover all its secrets.

Where the path forks turn right off the track to see the Nine Ladies. This Bronze Age stone circle is 33 feet in diameter and has an accompanying King's Stone a few yards away. Single stones are often found by such circles and are thought to represent the male symbol in Bronze Age fertility rites. The story goes, locally, that the Nine Ladies were village maidens who were turned to stone for dancing on the sabbath. The King's Stone was the fiddler, who suffered the same fate.

Retrace your steps and take the other fork, which crosses a fence to pass a tall stone tower erected in tribute to Earl Grey, the Prime Minister who carried the Reform Bill through Parliament in 1832.

Many paths cross the moor, but the most exhilarating is the one along the eastern edge, on which you are now walking. The panorama across the Derwent Valley is superb, as you can verify by leaving the path where the fence bends right and walking to the large boulder perched on the edge (viewpoint). Below sprawls Darley Dale, with the high moors above Chatsworth behind and to the left. Further along the path you should be able to pick out the distinctive shapes of Riber Castle and Crich Stand. One is a zoo, the other a lighthouse. Honest.

Return to the main path. After 300 yards you come upon the scant remains of a building and a few pine and birch trees near the edge. Just to the right of these, if you look carefully, is a long sheer drop where a quarry has eaten into the edge. My dog fell down here in 1980 when he was four - and lived!

When you reach the road turn right. At the next junction turn left if you want the Red Lion or Birchover Camping Barn (100 yards on the left, reached via a gap in the wall); turn right to continue on the main route.

After 100 yards turn left through the car park to the viewpoint beyond, then take the path dipping left. This bypasses the village to bring you out opposite the Druid Inn. Next take the narrow lane to the left of the pub, just beyond which is the access point for Rowter Rocks (viewpoint). This extraordinary maze of rock chambers, tunnels, steps and carved seats was thought by locals to be linked with druids

Rowter Rocks

Carving in Hermit's Cave

- hence the name of the inn - but is, in fact, the folly of one man, Thomas Eyre, an eccentric parson who carved out his own little utopia here in about 1700.

Carry on down the lane, leaving it where it swings sharp left, and continue ahead on the grassy track contouring the wooded hillside. The large gritstone crag across the valley is Cratcliffe Tor, a popular climbing ground. A little further over to the left is another rocky outcrop with two distinct pinnacles. In the fading light of dusk these pinnacles bear an uncanny resemblance to chimneys atop a crumbling ruin (well, they do if you have been in the pub till dusk,) which has led the rocks to be known locally as Mockbeggar's Hall. The Ordnance Survey labels them Robin Hood's Stride, as in legend the famous outlaw jumped from one to the other to avoid capture - a distance of 22 yards! I would have thought the Stumps a far more credible name as they are the length of a cricket pitch apart, but who am I to say?

A few yards past a ruined building the path crosses a stile and descends to the road, along which turn left. After 150 yards turn right up the track signposted Cliff Lane. Circle round behind the Stride to the far side to find the easiest way up. There is an excellent all-round view from beneath the pinnacles (viewpoint).

To visit Cratcliffe Tor, cross the track and walk along the topside of the wood. Turn to the right beyond the stile and descend into the trees. Hidden beneath an enormous yew tree is the Hermit's Cave, which is famed for the remarkable fourteenth century carving of the

27

The Youlgreave youth hostel

crucifixion adorning its back wall. The recess by its side was probably hollowed out at a later date to hold candles when the cave was used as a resting place by travellers on the Portway, an ancient road that ran close by.

Retrace your steps to the track, then head diagonally across two fields to a road. If bound for Elton turn left, then left again at the footpath sign after three quarters of a mile. The path follows a direct line across fields to the church, visible ahead. A gate with an accompanying signpost leads to a lane behind the church; this in turn leads to the main road where you turn left for the hostel. The Tea Room & Guest House is on the junction.

For the main route turn right. After 300 yards turn left and follow a delightful woodland path. Cross the tiny stream at the far side and double back right along a rising track. Having rounded the hill the waymarked path makes a bee-line for Youlgreave church. Turn right upon reaching the road, then left almost immediately to cross the River Bradford. Turn left then take the tarmac path ascending the hill to the village. Turn right along the main road for the hostel, which is cunningly disguised as the Co-op.

Anti-clockwise Directions   Youlgreave to Bakewell

Turn down Holywell Lane, branching left just past the chapel to descend the tarmac path into Bradford Dale. Cross the footbridge and walk up to the road. Turn right then left into the field. Turn left alongside a wall beyond the next stile until you reach a farm track. The way forward is now obvious, this path being part of the waymarked Limestone Way.

Having rounded the final hill, cross the tiny stream and double back to the stile leading into the wood. At the far side turn right along the road. After 300 yards follow the fieldpath, left, to Robin Hood's Stride [page 27]. (To visit the Hermit's Cave [page 27] cross the pasture above the wooded slope and turn right beyond the stile. Retrace your steps.)

Follow the track down to the road and turn left. After 150 yards ascend the path on the right to join the track into Birchover. [Rowter Rocks page 25]

Take the path across the road from the Druid Inn. Note the view left from the summit then turn right down the road and left at the junction. Turn left along the Stanton Moor Edge path at the National Trust sign. Follow this to the stile beyond the Earl Grey Tower. After visiting the Nine Ladies stone circle [page 25] follow the track to the road. Turn left to descend into Stanton in Peak.

Turn right opposite the war memorial, taking to fields beyond the school. A series of squeezer stiles beside gates show the line. Beyond the stone byre descend diagonally left past the wall corner to a stile beneath a large tree. Note Haddon Hall in the foreground. Bear left passing a solitary tree to a footbridge in the bottom right-hand corner. Now bear slightly right to the road.

Turn right up the hill, take the track opposite Dove House Farm, which is just before the sharp bend, and skirt the hill to a small wood. Bear right across the field to join the dyke but leave this when it swings right. Continue down to meet the river and road which you follow past the cricket pitch into Rowsley. (Caudwell's Flour Mill, just past the bridge, is worth a visit.)

Cross the main road and continue ahead. The road becomes a track leading through the fringe of Manners Wood to Bowling Green Farm, just past which you turn right into fields. At the next farm track descend left, taking to the fields again just before reaching the river. The path soon joins the riverbank and is followed into the showground. To find the hostel follow the map on page 15. (Bakewell town plan).

Stage 2: Youlgreave To Ilam Hall 17 miles

(Alternatives: Elton to Ilam Hall 12¹/₂ miles, YHA;
Youlgreave to Alstonefield 13 miles, B&B.)

It is true that 17 miles can seem an awful long way, especially if you are walking with children. However this is actually a fairly easy stage, mainly on smooth and level tracks where it is possible to work up a fair head of steam. If 17 miles is definitely out of your league, worry not, there are alternatives. If you are hostelling stay at Elton instead of Youlgreave, if looking for B&B then stay in Alstonefield. (All these alternatives are described.)

A steady climb out of Youlgreave over Harthill Moor takes you out of gritstone country and onto the limestone plateau, which is entered via Gratton Dale. You may admire some fine railway architecture as you chug along a disused railway line a short distance, before climbing a hill called Aleck Low to reach Biggin. The pub, with its expansive lawn, is the sort of village inn you dream of sitting outside on glorious sunny days. The afternoon is devoted to Dovedale and its tributary dales and some of the most spectacular limestone scenery in Britain.

As well as the pub in Biggin, there is a teashop in Milldale. Ilam has a palacial youth hostel and limited B&B. There are no shops. The nearest pub is the Izaak Walton Hotel, a ten minute walk, which is passed on the way in. There is also B&B and hotel accommodation at nearby Thorpe, or full facilities in Alstonefield.

Return to Holywell Lane and follow it down past the village hall to the river. Cross over and ascend steeply through a nick in the gorge into the field above. At the far end cross the minor road and walk up the track opposite as far as the gate, branching off here to ascend towards Mawstone Farm. You pass to the left of the farm buildings to join a track zig-zagging up into sparse woodland.

The track winds up through open fields, with superb views opening up on your left. Leave the track at the gate (just beyond where a signposted footpath crosses) and bear half left across the field. Cross the tree belt and continue beside a wall. Aim left of the plantation on

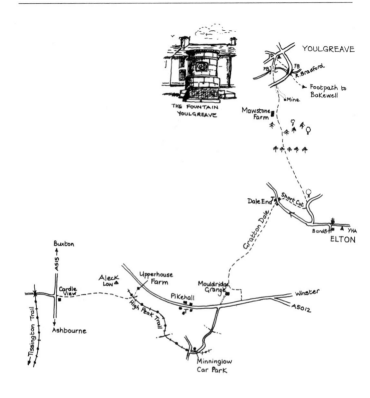

THE FOUNTAIN
YOULGREAVE

YOULGREAVE

PB
FB
Bradford
Footpath to
Bakewell
Mine
Mawstone
Farm
Dale End
Short Cut
Crofton Dale
BandB
YHA
ELTON
Buxton
A515
Cardle
View
Aleck
Low
Upperhouse
Farm
Mouldridge
Grange
Winster
Pikehall
A5012
High Peak Trail
Tissington Trail
Ashbourne
Minninglow
Car Park

Stage 2:
YOULGREAVE to ILAM HALL
(first section)

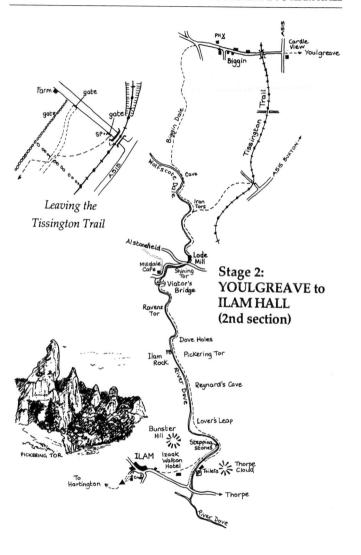

Leaving the
Tissington Trail

**Stage 2:
YOULGREAVE to
ILAM HALL
(2nd section)**

the skyline, cross the saddle and dip left, following the broken wall beneath brooding outcrops. Aim diagonally right beyond a fence stile, pass through three gateways and follow the wall on your left along the contour to a stile beneath an old quarry. Follow the track to the road and turn right (viewpoint). I always enjoy a breather here on this quiet lane which used to be a coaching road. I love to paddle in the horse troughs!

The signposted path going right at GR.218613 is a short-cut to Dale End. A series of easy to follow squeezer stiles then fence stiles lead to the road, where turn left. Walkers overnighting at Elton should follow the road to Dale End; they should *not* attempt the path through Oddo House Farm.

The Gratton Dale path begins at the phone box. Not very pretty to start with, but the scenery improves markedly beyond the old lime kiln. Just beyond a stand of conifers and opposite a re-entrant valley, cross to the other side of the broken wall for easier progress. After passing the junction with Long Dale the path sweeps up to the left, then rounds the wall on your right to meet the A5012. Turn right, then left along the Parwich road. After about a mile you come face to face with a most imposing and impressive limestone railway embankment.

The Cromford and High Peak Railway was opened in 1830 to link the Cromford Canal with the Peak Forest Canal at Whaley Bridge. It was a freight line carrying mainly limestone and coal. A passenger service did operate in summer for a time, but was never financially viable and was therefore soon discontinued. Steam locomotives were introduced in 1834 but did not completely replace horse-power until 1841. There were several inclines too steep for horses or engines, so stationary winding engines were used to pull the wagons up and lower them down the gradients.

The only portion of the line in operation today is the quarry branch from Dowlow to Buxton; the rest was purchased by Derbyshire County Council and the Peak Park Planning Board and converted to an amenity route for walkers, cyclists and pony trekkers. You join the High Peak Trail by turning right into Minninglow car park. You leave it about a mile later above Upperhouse Farm, having negotiated the incredibly tight Gotham Curve. I know it's easy for you, but just imagine the difficulties for a 200-yard-long steam train!

After 100 yards take the signposted path on the right. If there is an established line, follow it. If not, walk on a bearing of 300° to the top of the field. Locate the stile then follow the waymarked path over Aleck Low (all the highest hills in limestone country are 'Low') to the A515, emerging via the drive of the house called Cardle View. Having looked at the Cardle, whatever that is, cross over and follow the minor road opposite to Biggin, where a warm welcome awaits White Peak Wayfarers at the Waterloo (see pub guide) which has a campsite.

Continue to the junction, bear right for a few yards then follow the track down Biggin Dale. Pass the turn-off to Hartington, bear left to the next signpost and there turn right to continue down the dale. Bear left upon reaching the River Dove.

A faster, but not so attractive route, is to use the Tissington Trail. When you reach the railway bridge before Biggin ascend the embankment, turn left and chug along the old trackbed for 2 miles. The trail follows the line of the old Buxton - Ashbourne railway and joins the High Peak Trail near Parsley Hay. The line was engineered by Francis Stephenson and opened in 1899, forming part of a through route from London to Manchester. Passenger services ceased in 1954 although tourist excursions operated from Manchester and Sheffield until 1963. The Park Authority bought the line in 1968, grassed over the trackbed, demolished the stations and converted them to picnic sites and car parks. An 11$\frac{1}{2}$-mile stretch from Ashbourne to Hartington was opened in 1971, with a further 1$\frac{1}{2}$-mile stretch to Parsley Hay and the link with the High Peak Trail being completed the following year.

At the second road bridge climb down the embankment on the right to a gate, immediately entering the adjoining field. Walk down this, pass through a gateway in the broken wall on the left and approach the head of a dry valley. Descend this quiet, attractive and ever-deepening gorge until you meet the River Dove. Follow the river downstream to the road bridge below Shining Tor. (The old barn across the river was originally a lead smelting mill until the mines on Ecton Hill closed, when it was then adapted for corn milling. The water-wheel at the rear of the barn is still intact.)

Milldale

At this point there is a choice of routes. The quickest is over the bridge and left along the Milldale road. For the high-level alternative, if you have the time and energy, turn left, go through the green gate and follow the National Trust path avoiding the road. After quarter of a mile turn right as directed and ascend the hillside. Ignore the stiles at the summit and bear right along the outside of the wall. The purpose of all this climbing becomes apparent as you round Shining Tor to be greeted with the panorama up and down dale. As you stride along you can look down with scorn on your less brave companions shuffling along the road hundreds of feet below. You finally cross the wall before a zig-zag path leads you back down into the valley, rejoining the main route at Viator's Bridge.

The hamlet of Milldale is a convenient and popular starting point for visitors exploring the dales. Refreshments are available from Polly's Takeaway. If you are bound for Alstonefield you ascend the narrow lane opposite. This takes you directly into the village. Alternatively there is a steep footpath starting a couple of yards up the lane on the left, which rejoins it at the top. Alstonefield is without doubt one of the loveliest villages in the Peak, and in my opinion, in the entire country. Close by the village green there is a post office, store, tea-room and pub (see pub guide).

The mill which gave Milldale its name produced ochre pigment from locally mined iron ore. It was powered by the water channel running under the right-hand arch of the fine old seventeenth century packhorse bridge. On close inspection it is obvious that the parapets were added at a much later date. In *The Compleat Angler* by Izaak Walton and Charles Cotton, neither of whom could spell, Cotton recalls a journey on horseback with a companion referred to as Viator. Upon reaching this bridge a worried Viator hurriedly dismounted, horrified at the prospect of crossing such a narrow structure on horseback. Eventually, after much argument and complaint, he crawled across on hands and knees.

Having crossed Viator's Bridge (upright I hope) follow the riverside path through beautiful Dovedale. Without a doubt this is one of the grandest riverside walks in England, especially during the week when it isn't so crowded. The scene is best appreciated when illuminated by bright sunshine; the river sparkles and shimmers and the dull grey limestone is transformed to dazzling white.

Many impressive natural rock formations are encountered. The first is Ravens Tor, a huge limestone crag on the other side of the river. Next come the Dove Holes, a series of shallow caves with two large circular openings, the biggest 55 feet in diameter. These, like all the features, have been sculptured over many aeons by the inexorable passage of the Dove, which today cascades along over numerous tiny man-made weirs, which aerate the water and improve the fishing.

The dale begins to narrow as you approach Pickering Tor, noted for its five distinct pinnacles. The slopes become steeper and more densely wooded, their bases littered with scree. Rising sheer out of the water by the footbridge is the needle-shaped Ilam Rock, an imposing challenge to rock climbers. You immediately pass beneath Lion Head Rock. Look at its profile from beside the footbridge. If you can see the craggy head of a male lion it's because someone slipped something in your cereal this morning. Further on the dale narrows to such an extent that duckboards are needed.

A well trodden path on the left leads to Dovedale's outstanding feature - the natural arch in front of Reynard's Cave. At one time this was the cave entrance, but then the roof fell in and the river eroded away the debris to leave this splendid natural oddity.

Soon the path leaves the river to climb to the top of the predictably named Lover's Leap (viewpoint), though the only person ever known to have fallen over was a parson who, accompanied by his horse, plunged to his doom in 1761. His female companion survived because her hair caught in a tree and left her dangling until she was rescued. Lucky she was using firm hold hairspray! The view encompasses a wide stretch of Dovedale and overlooks other fancifully named features such as Dovedale Castle, Jacob's Ladder, Tissington Spires and the Twelve Apostles.

The path descends the other side of the hill to rejoin the river on the approach to the much photographed stepping stones which lie at the foot of a shapely little hill called Thorpe Cloud, an ancient reef knoll of richly fossilised coral. This is one of the few hills in the Peak District worthy of the name, for 'peak,' as a descriptive term, is a misnomer. The hills in these parts are more rounded than pointed and none compare with the mighty fells of Lakeland or the lofty mountains of Snowdonia. 'Peak' derives from the Old English word 'pec,' meaning hill. In Saxon times the area was called Peaclond and the inhabitants the Pecsaetna - the dwellers amongst hills. So Peak District literally means Land of Hill Dwellers, and not Land of Peaks.

The presence of limestone reef knolls (another is encountered further along) indicates that this area was once on the coast of a shallow sea. At this late stage of the day the prospect of climbing Thorpe Cloud, carrying a heavy pack, is about as inviting as toothache. Anyway, the view is much better from Bunster, the hill across the valley. A walk along the Bunster ridge makes a pleasant after dinner stroll, or you could leave it till after breakfast as you only have a short stage tomorrow. Or you could just leave it!

Either cross the stepping stones and walk along the road or continue on the left bank to the footbridge - both lead to the car park. Opposite the toilets is a footpath sign for Ilam. Branch right through the overspill car park and pass to the rear of the Izaak Walton Hotel (see pub guide). At the second stone stile the path bifurcates, the right fork climbing to the Bunster ridge, the left going to a kissing gate in the far corner and thence joining the road into Ilam via a farm track and a small gate just below a large tree stump.

Immediately upon entering the village you are confronted by a splendid ornate cross which was erected in 1840 by Jesse Watts Russell in memory of his wife. At about the same time he remodelled the village and rebuilt Ilam Hall, though a large part of the house of that period has since been demolished. Bear right at the cross then fork left as you approach the hall gates. Go through the gate on your left to approach the hall via the church.

Ilam church contains a number of interesting monuments, notably a remarkable sculpture in white marble by Sir Francis Chantrey which depicts the deathbed scene of David Pike Watts, surrounded by his family. On the opposite side in the south chapel is a shrine to St Bertram, a Mercian prince, who renounced his heritage after his family were killed and eaten by wolves. (His insurance policy did not cover such an eventuality.) He devoted the rest of his life to converting the local pagans to Christianity (and warning them of the dangers of being under-insured). His shrine has long been a place of pilgrimage and healing.

The bridge in the hall grounds, a well and a cave at the foot of nearby Beeston Tor are all named after Bertram, and the carvings on the old font are also thought to represent him.

Ilam Hall, as we see it today, was purchased by Sir Robert McDougal in 1934 and presented to the National Trust as a youth hostel. The trust have an information centre, giftshop and tea-room on the premises, whilst the hostel entrance is located beneath the arches.

Anti-clockwise Directions   Ilam Hall to Youlgreave

Walk past the church into the village. Bear left at the cross and take to the fields at the gate. Pass to the rear of the hotel and enter Dovedale.

Cross Viator's Bridge at Milldale and continue alongside the river following the road. Cross the bridge and continue along riverbank.

Turn right up the second side valley (Biggin Dale). At the signpost

39

next to the dew pond go left on the Hartington path and carry on at the next junction on the path to Biggin. Pass through the village to the A515. Cross over and follow the path over Aleck Low. Turn right along the High Peak Trail to Minninglow car park. Turn left along minor road then right along main road before taking the signposted path left into Gratton Dale. Cross to the other side of the broken wall opposite the re-entrant valley and stand of pines.

Either turn right along the road at Dale End then left at the junction, or turn left then right at the footpath sign for a shortcut across fields.

Turn left by the horse troughs, cross the stile and continue on this contour. Pass through two gaps then bear right to a third gap and head for a stile in the far corner. Follow the broken wall round to the right over the hill, then through a series of squeezer stiles. Cross a tree belt and bear left to the far corner, there joining a track which is followed down to Mawstone Farm. Pass to the right of the farm and descend to the road. Cross over, descend into Bradford Dale and climb the hill into Youlgreave. The hostel is cunningly disguised as a Co-op.

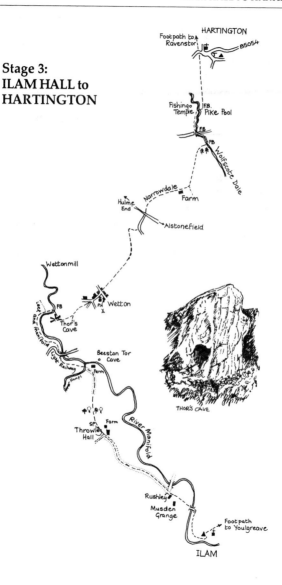

Stage 3:
ILAM HALL to
HARTINGTON

HARTINGTON

Footpath to
Ravenstor

B5054

Fishing
Temple

F.B.
Pike Pool

FB

FB

Wolfscote Dale

Narrowdale

Hulme
End

Farm

Alstonefield

Wettonmill

FB

Leek and Manifold
Light Railway

Thor's
Cave

Wetton

Beeston Tor
o Cave

Farm

Hamps

THOR'S CAVE

SP
Throwle
Hall

Farm

River Manifold

Rushley
Musden
Grange

Footpath
to Youlgreave

ILAM

Stage 3: Ilam Hall to Hartington   9 miles

(Alternative: Alstonefield to Hartington 14 miles.)

A day of high and low-level valley walking, through the beautiful Manifold and the upper dales of the Dove. There is a tea-shop at Wettonmill not far off-route and a lunchtime pub in Wetton (see pub guide). Hartington is a busy little village with a fine youth hostel, plenty of B&B and two pubs, as well as post office and shops.

Descend the steps at the front of the hall and turn right along the path known as Paradise Walk. By leaning over the railings you will notice two streams surging from tunnels beneath the path. The one on the left is the Manifold, the other the Hamps, both reappearing after following separate subterranean courses for several miles. The surface watercourses, which are normally dry, converge further along the Way at Beeston Tor. The disappearing act is not due to shyness but to the solubility of Carboniferous Limestone and the ease with which it is permeated. Both dry watercourses are encountered a little later on.

Further along Paradise Walk you come across a Saxon cross which was unearthed from the foundations of a house during the rebuilding programme of 1840, transplanted here and given a fancy name - the Battle Stone. When you reach the footbridge (not the one leading into Hinckley Wood) cross over and ascend the fields, via stiles, to the single track road by Rushley Farm. The path is faint and often indiscernable, so as a guide keep Musden Grange close by on your left as you climb.

A short distance down the road to the right the normally dry riverbed is spanned by Rushley Bridge, which usually manages to maintain a sizeable pool beneath it as though fulfilling its obligation to span water in spite of the peculiarities of limestone rivers. Our way, however, lies left and then immediately right along the lane to Throwley. The ruin in front of the farm is Throwley Hall, the seventeenth century home of the Meverells, whose family tomb can be seen in the south chapel of Ilam church. Pass through the farm behind the hall to a footpath sign. Go through two stiles then ascend the middle of the pasture to a ladder-stile. Descend the other side of the hill to another ladder-stile and a farm track. Ahead stands the massive limestone buttress of Beeston Tor; watch for climbers ascending its vertical 200-foot face.

The track passes Beeston Tor Farm and continues, as a metalled lane, to Weag's Bridge. If you wish to see the tor at close quarters and would like to inspect St Bertram's Cave it is possible to do so by backtracking along the riverbed, and you don't even need to take your boots off! During excavations in 1924 the Reverend G.H. Wilson discovered a hoard of Saxon coins believed to have been deposited in the cave in the ninth century. He hung around for several days, but no-one came to collect them, so he whipped them off to a museum. Lynx Cave, situated higher up the cliff, is so named because only the bones of lynx have been found there, whereas bones from numerous animals have been unearthed from other caves nearby. Perhaps only the lynx can jump that high?

Returning to the road you will notice a similar lane emerging from the Hamps Valley to run parallel with the one you are walking on. Why didn't they simply merge? The answer is that the other one is a railway - the Leek and Manifold Valley Light Railway which closed in 1934 and was macadamed over by Staffordshire County Council for the benefit of pedestrians and cyclists.

The old line once ran from Waterhouses, near Leek, through the valleys of the Hamps and Manifold to Hulme End, near Hartington, a distance of 9 miles. The track had a narrow gauge of 2 feet 6 inches, and the ornate open carriages were pulled by two engines called the E.R. Calthrop and the J.P. Earle (named after the engineers). As well as running a holiday passenger service the railway carried milk and dairy produce from the Ecton creamery and neighbouring farms. However, like many others the line never made a profit and so it closed down after only thirty years. A shame, for it must have been a delightful journey through the picturesque wooded valleys, with flowers wafting in the breeze at trackside and the river babbling past, even though it was underground and out of sight. If only those two small steam locomotives with their bright yellow Indian verandah coaches had been preserved, then this would surely have been one of the Peak's major tourist attractions.

Fishing Temple, River Dove

Cross the road at Weag's Bridge and continue along the trail for another mile - the car park was formerly Grindon station. Set impressively at the base of a towering crag up on the right is Thor's Cave, named after the Norse god of thunder. Before leaving the trail you could continue a further half mile to Wettonmill, where there is a tea-shop and campsite. Backtrack to the footbridge, and yes, you've guessed it, ascend the 300 or so feet to the cave. During the latter stages you have to negotiate more than a hundred steps, which is great fun. When you reach the top remove your rucksack before collapsing or you might squash your sandwiches (viewpoint).

The cave entrance is 30 feet high and 23 feet wide and when excavated yielded a Neolithic skeleton believed to be the last idiot to climb up here before you. When you have recovered continue around the base of the crag along a concessionary path leading to Wetton. Take the Alstonefield-Ilam road through the village, and at the sharp bend (round which you will find Ye Olde Royal Oak) go to the left of Manor House Farm. Shortly beyond the signpost to "Back of Ecton" take the diverted path right into the field. Fifty yards beyond the farm cross the wall on your right, go through the squeezer stile and continue with the wall now on your left. When this ends continue on the same line across the middle of the next four fields. The next stile is in the wall on your left. Continue 200 yards beyond where this ends to a stile just the other side a strip of trees. Walk parallel with these to the road, turn left and follow it to the junction.

Cross over and take the gated lane down Narrowdale, bypass the farm and turn sharp left at the bottom of the hill. After 100 yards you enter a walled track. Just before the fourth gate go to the right through a small dilapidated wooden gate and skirt the wood to a footbridge. This crosses the Dove at the top of Wolfscote Dale where the narrow dale temporarily widens into a broad meadow before continuing as an even darker ravine through densely wooded Beresford Dale.

This proximity of the Dove has close associations with those two piscatorial authors, Izaak Walton and Charles Cotton. The publication in 1653 of Walton's The Compleat Angler immortalised the Dove as a trout fishing stream - a reputation it holds to this day. His life-long friend, Charles Cotton, was born nearby at the now demolished Beresford Hall. Cotton, who was an even worse poet than Walton was a speller, added a second volume of fishy stories, one of which was the naming of Viator's Bridge mentioned earlier. He built a small retreat near the river where he and Izaak could relax and reminisce about the ones that got away. He recalls sitting outside on sunny mornings partaking of his favourite breakfast, which was a pipe of tobacco, before the pair of them would stroll, rods in hand, down to their favourite spot, nicknamed the Pike Pool (not after the species of fish but after the pillar of rock emanating from the murky depths of the river). Trout and grayling lurked here just waiting to be caught. The best view of it can be had by looking downstream from the new footbridge. The fishing temple stands on private ground on the Staffordshire bank and is inaccessible, though it can just about be glimpsed through the trees. Above the door is the inscription 'Piscatoribus Sacrum 1674' together with the friends' entwined initials.

Having once more emerged into the open the path leaves the river

Hartington Hall Youth Hostel

and crosses open meadow to a stile a few yards to the right of a gate. Across the track take the right-hand one of two stiles and continue into Hartington. Turn right into the square and right again at the phone box for the hostel, a charming Jacobean-style hall built in 1611.

Anti-clockwise Directions   Hartington to Ilam Hall

Take the path by the side of the public conveniences, cross the farm track and continue over meadow into Beresford Dale. Cross the ford then the footbridge at the top of Wolfscote Dale, following the overgrown path round the wood into Narrowdale. Turn right, pass the farm and walk along the lane to the road.

Take the minor road opposite, turn right into fields beyond the bend and follow the path into Wetton. Follow the track and concessionary path to Thor's Cave, descend to the valley floor and turn left along the trail.

Cross the road at Weag's Bridge, following the left-hand lane to Beeston Tor Farm. Continue on a rough track over the hill to Throwley Hall and down the lane to Rushley. Turn right into fields before the bridge to Ilam Country Park, turning right beyond the footbridge alongside the river to the hall.

To Wormhill

Footpath to Castleton

Miller's Dale

RAVENSTOR
Y.H.

River Wye

Chee Dale

A6 Buxton

Quarry

Viaduct F.B.

B6049

Slurry Pond

Deep Dale

to Buxton Y.H.

Cave

Blackwell

A6

Back Dale

Horseshoe Dale

A5270

Buxton

Jay-b

Stile

A515

Quarry

SP

Stage 4:
HARTINGTON to
RAVENSTOR

Earl
Sterndale
Inn

SP

Underhill

SP

SP

Crowdecote
Inn

Longnor

SP

Pilsbury Castle
Hills

Pilsbury

HARTINGTON HALL

River Dove

gated road

Pilsbury

HARTINGTON

pond

pump

Inn

Phone Box

Inn

Toilets

HARTINGTON

Ilam

Footpath
to Ilam

Stage 4:   Hartington to Ravenstor   16 miles

(Alternatives: Hartington to Buxton 11 miles;
Hartington to Tideswell 17$^{1/}$2 miles.)

A fairly long stage, especially for those bound for Tideswell. Buxton is a shorter alternative, but a diversion is necessary. Hostellers using the booking bureau may be diverted to Buxton should Ravenstor be fully booked, which it occasionally is in August. Backpackers also need to be diverted - to Blackwell, where B&B is also available.

The first part of the day is plain sailing, but further on you meet some fairly rugged country. Deep Dale and the Wye Dales are deep, wild and isolated ravines with stony paths which slow the pace, so don't dawdle on the first half. If you make Earl Sterndale before noon, and don't get delayed in the Quiet Woman, you should reach the end in plenty of time for dinner. Refreshments are hard to come by on this stage, though the Quiet Woman is perfectly situated for a lunchtime halt, but only light snacks are available. There is a cafe near Millers Dale station, and a pub by the river, but both come near the end of the stage. Ravenstor was voted the best hostel on the White Peak Way by charity walkers a few years ago and is a grand place. You need to walk back to Millers Dale for the pub (see pub guide). Tideswell is the biggest settlement since Bakewell and has every amenity, within reason. Buxton is, of course, a fairly large town.

A narrow gated lane leaves Hartington from the head of the duck pond and ascends the Dove Valley to the farming hamlet of Pilsbury. Midweek the road should be completely devoid of traffic, leaving you to enjoy your morning stroll in peace. The hilly ground on the right was once rich in lead and was extensively mined; an open adit (horizontal mine shaft) can still be seen near Ludwell Farm, beyond which the Lud Well, an underground spring, surfaces from beneath the road to join the Dove. From here on you are never far from the river, and on a clear sunny morning the valley makes a charming picture.

At Pilsbury leave the road at the sharp bend and continue ahead up the farm track to Pilsbury Castle Hills. Cross the stile just beyond and descend the rutted track to the signpost and stile at the bottom.

The path continues across pleasant water meadows, never far from the river, to reach the hamlet of Crowdecote via a farm track. The impressive peak in the distance is Parkhouse Hill, which along with its partner, Chrome Hill, forms the reef knoll mentioned earlier. The route takes you right up to and around these jagged peaks, affording excellent views from varying angles.

Turn left beyond the Packhorse Inn and in 70 yards a signpost marks the path to Glutton Bridge (a lovely name, that). This passes farm buildings following a straight course to another signpost at a crossroads of paths. Join the farm road going through the gate opposite and follow this for half a mile until you see a signpost for Earl Sterndale opposite a renovated cottage. Cross the field to a stile and then climb Hitter Hill, aiming left once above the trees. At the top locate the stile in the narrow field corner and continue over the summit (viewpoint) to the village, emerging from the rear of the pub onto the road (see pub guide).

Note the extraordinary inn sign, which depicts a headless woman. It is said that a former landlord had a nagging wife who was always showing him up in front of the customers. One day he was late home from the Longnor market so she dispatched several customers to go out and look for him. This was the final straw. On his return the angry and humiliated landlord commissioned the sign. His explanation was - 'If I can't have a quiet woman inside my house, I'll have her outside instead.' (I bet you think I made that up.)

Walk up the road past the church, rounding the tiny park, and continue to a disused quarry beyond which you clamber up through someones rockery (officially) to the path climbing steeply up the hill, aiming half-left. A little beyond the summit you meet a wide track running along the boundary of an enormous quarry. The footpath has been rerouted around this eyesore so turn left for quarter of a mile, following the sign for Chelmorton. The concrete bunker is not a toilet, even though it smells like one. It is actually there to prevent you being blown up during blasting times.

The quarrying of limestone and its associated minerals - fluorspar, baryte and calcite - is the only heavy industry flourishing inside the Peak District National Park. Naturally it is subject to strict control. It should, of course, be banned altogether, but people do have to make a living. The majority of the larger quarries are concentrated around Buxton and Wirksworth outside the park boundary. There can be no doubt that quarrying results in ugly disfigurement of the landscape, as you now bear witness, but nature somehow seems to compensate. In this case the compensation is the butterflies. Whenever I walk this track in summer there always seems to be dozens of them flitting along the ground. In one afternoon alone I identified the common blue, green-streaked white, red admiral and large tortoiseshell. There were others, but they refused to tell me their names. The company hires them to flit around and distract visitors from the damage being caused.

Cross the stile on the right at the far end of the quarry, head for the stile midway in the opposite wall, then keep to the field boundaries as signposted, finally leaving the Chelmorton path after crossing the railway bridge. Follow the wide farm track, which soon forks to the right through the farmyard, then continue down the drive to the road and turn left. Cross over at the far end of the lay-by and locate the stile concealed in the undergrowth below. Head diagonally left to a stile in the far corner, then descend into Horseshoe Dale. Head for the farm buildings on the roadside; the stile is at the side of the telephone poles. Cross the road and continue down the dale.

Horseshoe Dale merges into the magnificent untamed wilderness of Deep Dale where Black Dale joins from the left. (The Buxton Alternative starts here; see end of chapter for route description.) The path, like the scenery, is rugged, crossing limestone scree and slippery boulders interspersed with thick vegetation (including nettles so make sure your legs and other tender bits are covered). It would be wise to slow your pace. Anyway, there is no desire to hurry when surrounded by so much beauty. Wild flowers are abundant, particularly in the vicinity of Thirst House Cave (viewpoint) which you can follow back for quite a way.

It comes as something of a shock when, nearing the head of the dale, you stumble upon the outlying spoil heaps of Topley Pike Quarry, which has desecrated the upper reaches of this otherwise untainted valley. However nature compensates again here, for these old tips contain a network of warrens and if you sit quietly for a while the rabbits might come out and put on a show.

Keep straight on past the slurry pond, descend steeply and bear left along the path outside the boundary fence. Cross the A6 to the car park opposite and turn right on the bridleway running alongside the River Wye. Walkers bound for Ravenstor and Tideswell follow the river for about four miles, those bound for Blackwell branch off just before the footbridge in front of a line of cottages. (The route is described at the end of the chapter.)

The path crosses to the left bank as you enter the narrow confines of Chee Dale - so narrow, in fact, that in places you are forced to walk on stepping stones in the river. The path temporarily switches to the other bank, negotiates more stepping stones, then rounds the massive face of Chee Tor before climbing away to cross a tributary. As you return to the bank the dale begins to open out and the jungle is temporarily left behind. You pass the footbridge where the Blackwell Alternative rejoins the main route and continue on to a road. However, instead of joining the road you now double back left, up to Miller's Dale station. Follow the Monsal Trail over the dizzy heights of the viaduct and continue for a mile before descending the steps on the left, opposite the sign for Priestcliffe Lees Nature Reserve. This brings you out more or less opposite the rear entrance to the hostel. The track winds up to the house, which stands in splendid isolation in its own grounds.

The Buxton Alternative

Leave the route in Horseshoe Dale, at the junction with Back Dale. Go through the metal gate and climb the switchback path, pausing at the top to admire the view along the length of Deep Dale. Go through the gate and head either straight across the middle, or round the left-hand edge of the field (depending on circumstances) to a gate in the opposite wall. Bear right to the far corner where an enclosed track brings you to the King Sterndale road. Follow this to the right for a few yards before turning left opposite the Old Vicarage. Cross the wooden stile and walk up the field close by the fence on your left. Cross over the wall and continue alongside the wood, through a gap stile and on towards the farm buildings ahead. Pass to the right, turn right along the road for a few yards and take the signposted path left,

51

which soon joins a farm track. When this peters out continue ahead alongside the wall on your right.

Follow the track up through the farming hamlet of Staden, going straight on at the crosstracks. A good view over Buxton is soon revealed. Descend into the walled green lane, cross the track at the bottom and ascend towards the railway. Pass under the viaduct and descend gradually to the road. Buxton's youth hostel is directly in front of you across the A515. The entrance is on Harpur Hill Road.

Retrace your steps to King Sterndale and turn left towards the church, where you can see the graves of the Pickford family, founders of the famous haulage firm. Take the stile on the right just before the church and cross the fields back into Deep Dale, rejoining the main route just north of Thirst House Cave.

The Blackwell Alternative

Instead of crossing the footbridge turn right by the side of the shed and ascend to cross the bridge spanning the disused Midland Railway, which may soon be opened as a steam railway by the Peak Railway Society. Climb the stile on the left and haul yourself up to the 270-foot summit of Plum Buttress - the highest limestone face in Derbyshire. The view down, depending on your equilibrium, is either heart-stopping or (as in my case) terrifying.

Leave the edge to cross the stile, immediately bearing left for the next one beside the forlorn tree. Now head up the field to a stile on the right of the ruinous building, then bear left up the hillside following the wall to the corner where you join a walled track leading to Blackwell. The campsite office is a short distance down the road.

Walk up the drive of Blackwell Hall (B&B) and continue through the farmyard on the wide track. Turning into a field the path hugs the wall on the left, then continues straight ahead to a barely distinguishable stile in the wall. Keep close to the broken wall, skirting the edge for glorious views down Chee Dale before descending steeply to a fence. Follow the fence for a short way until you reach the footbridge at the bottom where you rejoin the main route some two miles short of Ravenstor. It is therefore about 13 miles from Blackwell to Castleton by the main route. For an even shorter day you can cross the main route and follow the Wormhill Alternative, described at the beginning of the next stage.

Anti-clockwise Directions   Ravenstor to Hartington

Cross the footbridge over the Wye, ascend the steps to the Monsal Trail and turn right. At the far end of the platform of Miller's Dale station descend the path on the left then turn right along the riverbank. Cross the A6 and enter Topley Pike Quarry. Follow the path left of the works into Deep Dale.

Cross the road and bear right, climbing the side of Horseshoe Dale to a stile, then head diagonally left to the main road. Pass through Brierlow Grange, cross the railway and follow the signposted path around field edges to the quarry track where turn left. Turn right opposite the shelter and descend to the road, turning left into Earl Sterndale.

Take the path from the rear of the pub, descend Hitter Hill and turn left along a farm track. Go straight across at the crosstracks and continue into Crowdecote. Pass the inn and turn left across meadows into Pilsbury, there following the gated road into Hartington.

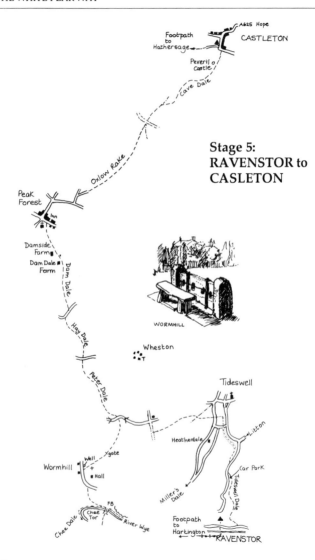

A625 Hope
CASTLETON

Footpath
to
Hathersage

Peveril o
Castle

Cave Dale

Stage 5:
RAVENSTOR to
CASLETON

Oxlow Rake

Peak
Forest

Inn

Damside
Farm
Dam Dale
Farm

Dam Dale

Hay Dale

WORMHILL

Peter Dale

Wheston

Tideswell

Litton

Heatherdale

Car Park

Wormhill

Well   gate

Hall

Miller's
Dale

Tideswell
Dale

FB

Chee
Tor

River Wye

Chee Dale

Footpath
to
Hartington

RAVENSTOR

Stage 5:   Ravenstor to Castleton   9 miles

(Alternatives: Buxton to Castleton, via Wormhill, 14 miles;
Tideswell to Castleton 8 miles.)

Castleton is a lively tourist-oriented village which is well worth exploring if you have the time, and as this is a short stage it should be possible to arrive by mid-afternoon in order to do just that. Whichever route you walk, today is one of contrasting dales, from shallow valleys to deep-riven ravines, but with a splendid airy climb across grassy moor inbetween. There is a convenient lunchtime pub in Peak Forest, which also has a post office cum general store. Castleton has a wealth of pubs, cafes and shops.

The Wormhill Alternative

Those heading to Castleton from Buxton might prefer to use the old route, a managable 14 miles as opposed to nearly 20 miles via Tideswell.

Upon reaching the footbridge in Chee Dale (grid ref 127735) where the Blackwell alternative rejoins the route, double back left and ascend the hillside to Wormhill. Turn left along the road past the grounds of Wormhill Hall, then turn right down the lane leading to the Parish Church of St Margaret. Before doing this you may wish to walk on to the green to view the stocks and the well, which was erected (somewhat belatedly) in 1875 in memory of James Brindley, the canal builder, who was born nearby at the farming hamlet of Tunstead in 1716. Although almost totally illiterate, Brindley became the pioneer of canal building in Britain, constructing some 400 miles of waterway in total.

Over the August bank holiday this fountain is decorated in accordance with the ancient Derbyshire custom of well dressing. The worship of wells dates back to pagan times, though the art of decoration originated at Tissington in the seventeenth century, following a severe drought through which the village springs never ran dry.

For the decoration a sunken panel, containing a layer of soft clay,

James Brindley Memorial Well, Wormhill

serves as the base into which a design is pricked and then pegged. Then, by pressing in hundreds of vividly coloured, and overlapping flower petals, plus moss, lichens, bark etc., a picture of remarkable clarity and realism is created. The scenes depicted are normally of a religious or biblical nature, and upon their completion a service is held to bless the well. Because only natural materials are used the pictures have a limited lifespan of about a week, but during this period thousands of extra visitors descend on the dozen or so villages which practise the art throughout the summer.

The Wormhill Well traditionally depicts a church or cathedral. It always amuses me the way the village street is bedecked with bunting improvised from different coloured fertilizer bags. Why waste money on flags?

Before leaving Wormhill a quick circuit round the church would not go amiss as it is a charming old building in an attractive arboreal setting. The lane winds past the vicarage and there you will see a signpost. Enter the field by rounding the wall then head for the solitary hawthorn tree in the distance, beside which is a stile. Across the next field enter a narrow walled lane, soon bearing right at a small wooden gate and stile to continue between limestone walls on the winding descent to a second gate, through which the path drops steeply to the road. Cross over and enter Peter Dale by the Nature Reserve notice board, rejoining the main route.

Ravenstor to Castleton via Tideswell

Descend to the river and follow the road towards Litton Mill for half a mile before turning into Tideswell Dale just past the car park. At the far end follow the avenue of trees beyond the car park and turn right along the road.

Take the path just past the sewage plant, bear right and climb parallel with the road till a stile left brings you onto a farm track. Keep right at the fork, cross the road, pass the pinfold on the left and continue into Tideswell.

Just before the Horse and Jockey (see pub guide) turn left up the narrow ginnel called Primrose Lane (unless you wish to look round the village first and perhaps stock up with food - the butcher's pork pies are out of this world. The church - the Cathedral of the Peak - is worth a visit, too). At the top of the lane take the stile opposite, ascend close to the wall on your right, cross a farm track and continue as before - the path is easily identified by a line of prominent squeezer stiles. At the foot of the slope turn right along the farm track to the road junction. Turn left to descend steeply to the valley bottom. Turn right into Peter Dale beside the Nature Reserve notice board.

Peter Dale is shallow, in complete contrast to the Wye Dales, and noted more for its varied flora than its rock scenery. Stony at first the path soon broadens into a wide swathe of grass, leading to the minor road separating Peter Dale from Hay Dale.

Further into Hay Dale you will come upon an old lead mine. If you climb to the upper level you can see the entrance to the mine, which has wagon rails partly intact. An avenue of trees leads to a grassy track, which you follow right for 150 yards before crossing a wall-stile on your left into Dam Dale. You are now over 1,000 feet above sea level, climbing steadily northwards towards the highest point on the limestone uplands. As you can see the landscape is becoming ever more bare and devoid of trees, the soil being too thin and poor to support them in any great number.

Go through the gate by Dam Dale Farm and on to the stile in the left-hand corner. Keep this line over the brow of the hill ahead and pass to the right of the solitary house before turning left to join the metalled lane through Damside farmyard, which is followed out to the main road at Peak Forest, emerging next to the church and opposite the Devonshire.

A loophole in eighteenth century ecclesiastical law gave the local vicar the right to issue marriage licences without banns, which meant he could marry eloping couples on speck, day or night. Naturally Peak Forest was known as the Gretna Green of Derbyshire, but a law passed in 1754 restricted the practice and gradually it ceased altogether, which is not surprising. No offence, but there are far more lively places to spend a honeymoon than here!

Walk up Church Lane to Old Dam and turn right along Old Dam Lane. Take the next turning on the left towards a farm. Turn sharp right and then ascend the track, at first through trees, following the line of Oxlow Rake, an old lead vein. Higher up on the open moor, in the land of the lapwing and curlew, the path crosses the rake and continues by a wall to a crosstracks. Carry straight on, bearing half-right across the centre of the field. Descend into the dip and fork right to enter Cave Dale via a small metal gate. The smooth, gently descending path soon becomes steep, slippery and stony, but improves in the lower reaches when Peveril Castle comes into view.

William Peveril built the castle shortly after the Norman Conquest, following his appointment as bailiff of the royal manors in North Derbyshire. In other words his job was to stop the peasants poaching the king's deer. He got this lucrative post, not because of his skill as a gamekeeper, but because he was William the Conqueror's illegitimate son. The keep and gatehouse were added during the reign of Henry II; but by 1400 the castle was strategically of no further importance and was left to fall into ruin. Now in the care of the Department of the Environment the remains can be visited for a small fee, the entrance is next to the hostel.

Quite unexpectedly you now find yourself in the middle of Castleton, close to the youth hostel. The village owes its popularity with tourists to its four show caves - Speedwell, Treak Cliff, Blue John and Peak Cavern. It is situated on the geological dividing line between the White Peak and the Dark Peak, where limestone gives way to gritstone. Water flowing off the impervious grit has permeated the porous limestone to create these vast underground draining systems, which were first opened and exploited by lead miners in the eighteenth century.

It was during mining operations in Treak Cliff Cavern that the now famous Blue John fluorspar was first discovered. This is the rarest and most beautiful of our natural minerals and, due to its scarcity, is used solely for jewellery and ornamentation, examples of which can be seen in the village gift shops.

A new series of inner caves was discovered as late as 1926 when miners in search of further deposits of Blue John blasted a link between Treak Cliff Cavern and Blue John Mine on the other side of the hill. These new caves were found to contain some of the most remarkable stalactite and stalagmite formations yet seen in Britain. If it is your intention to visit one of the show caves I would recommend Treak Cliff Cavern as being the most interesting.

Evening strollers should head westwards out of the village to view Winnats Pass. A wide grass verge provides easy walking right to the top of this spectacular gorge.

Anti-clockwise Directions   Castleton to Ravenstor

Bear right out of Market Place and take the signposted path into Cave Dale. Go straight over the farm track along the right-hand path beside a wall. Cross Oxlow Rake and take the right-hand path alongside the rake.

Follow the road to Old Dam, turn left down Church Lane to the main road. Take the lane opposite the Devonshire Arms, walk through Damside Farm, then left and right behind Mill House and on to Dam Dale Farm. Here you enter Dam Dale.

At the far end turn right along the track for 150 yards, then cross the stile on your left to enter Hay Dale. Continue through Peter Dale to the road, turn left up the hill, right onto a farm track then left over a signposted stile into fields after 250 yards. Follow the path to the signpost at the top of the hill. Now continue on the same line,

59

following a series of prominent squeezer stiles, across a farm track and into Tideswell. Cross the road and descend Primrose Lane, turning left at the bottom for the village or right to continue the walk.

Go straight over the junction along a farm track for quarter of a mile. Cross the stile on the left of the gate and descend gradually to the road, where you turn right. Follow the avenue of trees into Tideswell Dale, turning right along the lane by the river to reach the hostel.

Winnats Pass

Stage 6: Castleton to Hathersage   14 miles

The highlight of today's stage is an exhilarating traverse of the ridge separating the Hope Valley from the Vale of Edale, together with the ascent of Win Hill, one of the best viewpoints on the walk. A veritable walk on the wild side, which ends with a relaxing stroll along the banks of the River Derwent.

There is a lunchtime halt at the Cheshire Cheese (see pub guide) and a tea shop in the Garden Centre at Shatton. Hathersage has a good choice of pubs, cafes and shops, along with a youth hostel, campsite and B&B.

Peak Cavern lies a short distance off the route out of Castleton, so if you have not already visited the impressive cave entrance we shall start by doing so. Walk down the narrow street at the side of the hostel then, having crossed the bridge, branch left beside Peakshole Water on the footpath leading to the huge yawning mouth of the cave. This is strikingly situated at the base of a sheer precipice, but somewhat marred by the recent erection of a wooden facade. The impregnability of Peveril Castle can be fully appreciated from here.

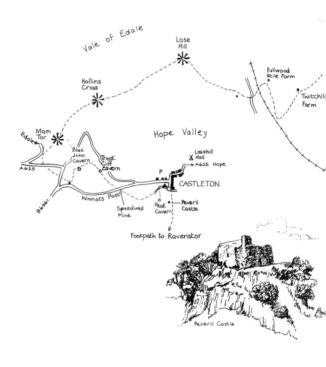

Peveril Castle

On the way back bear left, then turn left again on the path up Goosehill which soon becomes a stony track leading to a gate. Contour the hill along the top side of the wall until you meet the road through Winnats Pass by Speedwell Cavern. This former lead mine is unique in that visitors are ferried by boat along an illuminated canal to reach the caves. Take the path opposite, cross a wall-stile and head for Treak Cliff Cavern, which you can see on the hillside ahead. Climb the steps to the rear of the cavern and follow the public

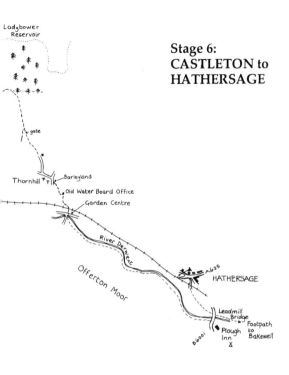

Stage 6:
CASTLETON to HATHERSAGE

footpath to the right. This skirts the cliff, presenting an excellent view of the landslip on Mam Tor, the continual denudation of which has forced the permanent closure of the old main road at its base. This famous 'Shivering Mountain' is composed of alternative layers of hard Millstone Grit and soft bands of shale, and it is the erosion of the shale that causes the slides.

Having rounded the hill, cross the stile and bear right to pass in front of the Blue John Cavern, and continue to ascend the waymarked path. Turn right on reaching the wall in front of a farm and cross a couple of fields to a road, across which the path bears half-right to another road. Ascend the pasture opposite and then climb the stepped path to the 1,696-foot summit of Mam Tor (viewpoint), the highest point on the White Peak Way.

The grandest view lies northwards over the Vale of Edale to the towering ramparts of the Kinder Plateau, a formidable barrier spreading across the horizon. The Pennine Way appears as a brown ribbon threading its way up Grindsbrook Clough from Edale village in the valley bottom. At weekends a constant stream of tiny figures, easily identified by their brightly coloured anoraks, can be seen moving up and down this track. They look like miniature cars on a distant motorway.

Kinder Scout is roughly 300 feet higher than Mam Tor, yet this minimal difference in elevation has a profound effect on local weather conditions. On several occasions I have walked this ridge and enjoyed perfect weather, whilst across the valley the moorland plateau has been enveloped in cloud. Many people, out for a leisurely stroll on a glorious sunny day, have found themselves suddenly stranded amongst the peat hags lost in swirling mist. It can be a frightening experience. It is not only the ill equipped and inexperienced day-trippers who keep the Mountain Rescue team busy, even parties of armed forces recruits have succumbed to the perils of Kinder and Bleaklow in bad weather. Mind you, trouble of this nature usually only befalls the unwary. A wise person anticipates the likelihood of adverse conditions in advance and prepares accordingly. In such circumstances always rely on your compass and a pre-planned escape route off the hill, *not* on your sense of direction and blind faith. The former, if used properly, will never let you down, the latter could cost you your life. However, the weather is not always dismal, it is just unpredictable. For the rambler seeking solitude there is no place finer than these vast, empty Pennine moors, most of which are covered by access agreements which give you the freedom to explore at will. Though the landscape is bleak and sombre in appearance, one may find true peace up here, the kind only experienced in harmony with nature in the raw, as the wild wind blows across the heather and the cotton grass. Hardy sheep, an occasional mountain hare and the

Mam Tor

raucous grouse are your only likely companions. The austere moorlands of Kinder and Bleaklow are good places, friendly places, providing you give them the respect their lofty position demands.

If you descend due south from the summit to the fence you get an excellent close up view of the landslip. From Mam Tor the ridge descends to its lowest point at Hollins Cross, where a memorial cairn stands at the intersection of the ridgeway and the old coffin track between Edale and Castleton. (No, it isn't used to convey expired hikers brought down from Kinder, it belongs to the time before there was a church in Edale.)

Following a stiff climb up Barker Bank the way levels out. At the next path crossing the ridge, cross the stile in the fence on your left and continue, beginning with the short, but steep, scramble up Back Tor. The River Noe, a road and the Sheffield - Manchester railway run in close proximity through the Vale of Edale, and during your time on the ridge it is almost certain you will see a train. Meanwhile, on the other side in the Hope Valley, Castleton is gradually left behind and you draw level with Hope. The most outstanding, and the most unpleasant landmark is the ever-smoking chimney of the cement works, built before the Peak District National Park opened.

The summit of Lose Hill boasts an unusual cairn topped with an inscribed plate, naming all the surrounding features and giving their distance and bearing. However, at an exposed 1,563 feet it is normally too cold and windy to spend over long searching out the various landmarks, so concentrate your attention eastwards to the distinctive peak of Win Hill which is our next target (unless your next target is the Cheshire Cheese on the Hope - Edale road down below. See pub guide).

An improved path drops steeply from the summit to a stile, beyond which bear left and continue down the long eastern arm of the ridge, eventually following a hollow-way between trees to join a track. Follow this round a right-hand bend to the main road. Continue for a quarter of a mile to the pub, or turn sharp left here to carry on to Hathersage.

Cross the River Noe and walk up the narrow lane as far as Fullwood Stile Farm. Here you turn right, bypassing the farm on the right, to a stile beside a gate. Walk along the top of the field parallel with the railway, soon to enter a tree-shaded lane. Leave this where it bends to the right under the railway bridge and carry straight on. Follow the track round to the left and ascend to Twitchill Farm beyond which the serious climbing begins. Scramble steeply up to the signpost before continuing on a more moderate incline towards the summit.

The rocky crest comes into view when you reach the heather-clad moor above the tree-line. Crows circling above the boulders indicate the absence of live human beings or the presence of dead ones. You may also startle a mountain hare into flight. These are much easier to spot in winter (unless there is snow on the ground when they sport a white coat). An immaculate Pennine vista unfolds as you breast the ridge, and a little higher up the twin arms of Ladybower Reservoir come into view, set amidst a forest of conifers.

It must be about lunchtime, so drop your pack and find a sheltered place amongst the rocks where you can eat your sandwiches and drink in the view (viewpoint). Looking back you can see all that you have accomplished so far today, from Castleton up to Mam Tor and along the ridge to Lose Hill. There is a story that in the seventh century two armies met here to do battle, a bit like mods and rockers did at Southend in the sixties. They made camp on opposite sides of the valley and the eventual victors named their camp Win Hill, t'other lot had to make do with Lose Hill.

Ladybower is the last in a chain of three large reservoirs built in the Upper Derwent Valley to supply water to Sheffield, Nottingham, Derby and Leicester. During its construction just before the war, two villages - Ashopton and Derwent - were submerged; and in times of exceptional drought (as in 1989) the water level drops sufficiently to reveal the ruins, an occurence that attracts sightseers by the thousand. The other two reservoirs - Howden and Derwent - were built at the turn of the century and were used by the Dambusters Squadron during the Second World War to perfect the technique which led to the destruction of the Ruhr dams in Germany. The film recounting the story of this epic raid was shot on location here.

Descend from the OS column to a ladder-stile, then carry straight on down through sparse woodland to a fence. Follow this to the right along an extremely pleasant green path which soon leaves the plantation to contour the hillside overlooking Bamford (viewpoint). The Derwent has its source on the spongy morass of Bleaklow, from where it flows south-east for a mere 4 miles before its capture and imprisonment by the Water Authority. It is then released from beneath the wall of Ladybower Dam to continue its journey south to freedom. It is possible to observe its course through the valley by following the line of trees hugging its banks.

In under half a mile you emerge from between banks of gorse to see a wooden gate a few yards down the hill. Go through this and descend into Thornhill, bearing left at the first road junction. Walk past the chapel and turn right by the phone box, then take the path beyond Barleyland, the last house on the left. This brings you out behind the one-time offices of the Derwent Valley Water Board. Walk round to the front of the building and take the stile opposite the entrance. Stick close to the hedge on your right until you are confronted by the railway, then bear left and follow the embankment to a tunnel. Walk through this and then cross the car park of the High Peak Garden Centre to emerge on the A625. This garden centre has a tea-shop and an excellent outdoor shop called Hitch n' Hike, should you need a new pair of socks. Follow the minor road opposite to cross the Derwent. Almost immediately you will see the stile on your left. The path at first follows a fence through woodland, but soon emerges beside the river into open meadow bounded on the right by the rounded slopes of Offerton Moor.

The Derwent is next bridged by the road at Leadmill 2 miles downstream, and it is here that you interrupt your riverside journey to divert to Hathersage for the night. Cross the bridge and squeeze through the stile in the wall on the left, then follow the fence across fields to join a lane leading under the railway viaduct into the village. Turn left along the main road for 150 yards for the hostel.

HATHERSAGE

Should you fancy an evening stroll, I strongly recommend a visit to the church. Walk up the main road past the George Hotel and take the path behind the Nat West Bank. Bear left and after a few yards take the path on the right ascending to the church.

Situated between two stumps of yew in front of the porch is the 11-foot-long grave of Little John, a native of Hathersage before he joined up with Robin Hood. After burying Robin at Kirklees Priory he returned to Hathersage to live out his days in peace. For many years his cap and longbow hung in the church, but were removed to Cannon Hall near Barnsley and were subsequently lost. Excavation of the grave in 1784 revealed a thigh bone thirty inches long, indicating the man was over seven feet tall. On view inside the church are the brasses of the Eyre family, builders of many of the big old halls dotted about the area.

When Henry Nussey proposed to his sister's best friend he was politely turned down. Undaunted he plighted his troth elsewhere, this time with more success. About the same time he got married he secured the position of Vicar of Hathersage, but before taking up the post he went on honeymoon. Whilst he was away his sister Ellen moved into the vicarage (which is situated behind the church and now does B&B) and invited her best friend down to help get the house in order. So it was that in 1845 Charlotte Brontë spent three weeks at

PLAN OF HATHERSAGE
(with emphasis on the location of watering holes).

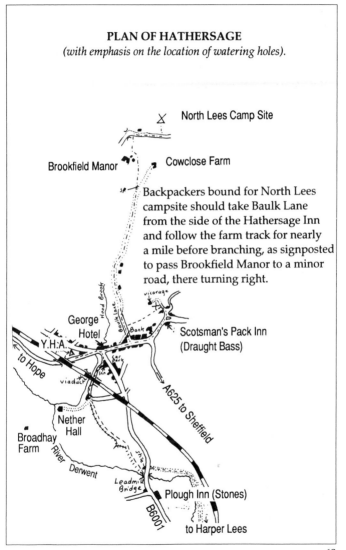

North Lees Camp Site

Brookfield Manor

Cowclose Farm

Backpackers bound for North Lees
campsite should take Baulk Lane
from the side of the Hathersage Inn
and follow the farm track for nearly
a mile before branching, as signposted
to pass Brookfield Manor to a minor
road, there turning right.

vicarage

George
Hotel

Y.H.A.

Scotsman's Pack Inn
(Draught Bass)

to Hope

viaduct

A625 to Sheffield

Nether
Hall

Broadhay
Farm

River Derwent

Leadmill
Bridge

B6001

Plough Inn (Stones)

to Harper Lees

69

The Plough Inn

the vicarage up to her elbows in detergent, just one year before the publication of *Jane Eyre*. It does not take an awful lot of detection to deduce where she got the name 'Eyre' from, nor to guess the identity of the village Morton or who inspired the character of St John Rivers.

If you leave the churchyard by the main entrance and descend to the road you will be pleasantly surprised to discover Charlotte's local, the Scotsman's Pack (see pub guide). You can make the return journey by road if it is dark and you are scared of crossing graveyards at night.

Anti-clockwise Directions   Hathersage to Castleton

Take the road opposite the George Hotel, branching right in front of the Little John Inn. Cross the stile beside Nether Hall and follow the farm track, then the path, to the road. Cross Leadmill Bridge, turn right and follow the riverbank for 2 miles to Shatton.

Cross the High Peak Garden Centre car park, pass through the tunnel and turn left. Walk to the rear of the old Water Board building, cross the track and ascend the path to Thornhill. Turn right, then left at the phone box and right again up Townhead Lane. Follow the path beyond the last house up onto the shoulder of Win Hill. Bear right beyond the small wooden gate to join a sunken track which soon becomes a very pleasant green path affording splendid views. Fork left approaching the wood, then left again for the final assault on the summit.

Head west from the summit and after about 200 yards take the first fork left. Descend through Twitchill Farm to the road. Continue ahead along the lane, branching left to the Coach House, beyond which continue the Way across fields to Fullwood Stile Farm. Turn left down the lane, cross the river and in 50 yards turn sharp right to begin the ascent of Lose Hill.

Descend the steps from the summit of Mam Tor, cross the stile on your left and descend the field to the road. Once over the road bear left, cross over the next road and bear left again. Pass in front of the Blue John Mine and round the hill to Treak Cliff Cavern. Continue on to the Speedwell Mine at the foot of Winnats Pass. Cross the road and follow the footpath alongside the wall into Castleton.

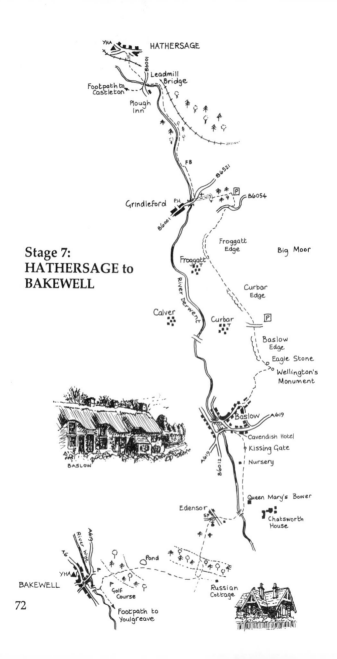

YHA HATHERSAGE

B6001

Leadmill
Bridge

Footpath to
Castleton

Plough
Inn

FB

B6521

Grindleford PH

B6001

B6054

Froggatt
Edge

Big Moor

Froggatt

River Derwent

Curbar
Edge

Calver

Curbar P

Baslow
Edge

Eagle Stone

Wellington's
Monument

**Stage 7:
HATHERSAGE to
BAKEWELL**

BASLOW

Baslow A619

Cavendish Hotel

Kissing Gate

Nursery

B6012

A619

Queen Mary's Bower

Edensor

Chatsworth
House

River Wye A619

A6

YHA P

Pond

Russian
Cottage

BAKEWELL P

Golf
Course

Footpath to
Youlgreave

72

Stage 7:   Hathersage to Bakewell   13 miles

The day starts with one of the loveliest stretches of the River Derwent, followed by a splendid walk along the rim of a gritstone edge, with extensive views throughout. Then, as a grand finale, comes a stroll through the landscaped magnificence of Chatsworth Park. The isolated Grouse Inn (see pub guide) might come too early for a lunchtime halt, in which case Baslow has several pubs to choose from. There are tea rooms in both Baslow and Edensor, and a range of shops in Baslow.

Take the lane on the right of the Little John Inn. Pass under the railway then round a left-hand bend to a solitary house, Nether Hall, just beyond which is a stile. Follow the farm track and then the fence to the main road at Leadmill Bridge. Cross over and follow the lane to Harper Lees. Go through the kissing gate on the right of the cattle grid and bypass the house to join the grassy track beyond. This soon rejoins the river, which you now follow for 2 miles to the road at Grindleford Bridge.

As you amble along, dreaming - if this is your last day - of how nice it will be to sleep in your own bed again, scan the mid-stream boulders for the white-breasted dipper bobbing up and down. Watch also for the tiny wren flitting in front of you from tree to tree, and for the blue flash of the kingfisher. There are ducks, too, and majestic trees and perhaps big dollops. Is there no finer way to start the day?

Cross the road and ascend the track beside the church. Just before reaching the farm turn left, as signposted, into Hay Wood. Follow the path up through this lovely birchwood, ignoring all intersecting paths. At the top the path bears right to join a good track just below the summit. Pass below the car park, down into the dip to ford a stream, then up the other side to the road where you turn right.

The track beyond the white gate leads on to Froggatt Edge where, almost immediately, you are confronted with an expansive panorama - a foretaste of what is to come. You don't really meet the rim until you have negotiated a kissing gate that I guarantee will cause an argument between you and your backpack as to who has right of way.

At an undefined point Froggatt Edge becomes Curbar Edge, and it

The Eagle Stone

is along here where some of the best climbs in the Peak District are to be found, so do not be too alarmed if a demented scream of 'Giz some bloody slack' rents the air from somewhere down below.

When you decide that it is time for elevenses, choose a comfortable-looking boulder close to the edge with a view of the valley and, providing it is not too windy, spread the map out on your knee. As an exercise in map reading, try to relate the features you see before you to those same features on the map; or, vice versa, pick an object or symbol from the map and then try and locate it. Having done that you can then not complain that the White Peak Way wasn't educational. I know someone who once spent minutes scanning the hills above Stoney Middleton through binoculars for an object which turned out to be a crumb from his gingernut biscuit.

After about 2 miles the path descends slightly to cross the minor road at Curbar Gap before continuing along Baslow Edge towards the Eagle Stone, a weathered block of grit that has withstood the forces of erosion and graffiti better than the surrounding deposits. Once, the young bucks of Baslow used to bring their girlfriends up

74

onto the moor and impress them by climbing this stone. Nowadays they take them for a spin in the Porsche.

Numerous rock formations similar to the Eagle Stone litter the High Peak moors, some of them weathered into the most fantastic shapes and given highly descriptive names (Salt Cellar, Cakes of Bread, Toad's Mouth, Wheel Stones, Manilow's Nose). Nearly all command excellent views and hence are marked on OS maps.

From the Eagle Stone stroll across to Wellington's Monument (viewpoint). Straight in front of you lies Chatsworth Park, with the 'Palace of the Peak' at its centre. You can sometimes see the Emperor Fountain spurting into the sky above the treetops. When going full blast it throws a jet of water 290 feet into the air, making it the highest fountain in Europe.

The monument to the Duke of Wellington stands 10-feet-tall and was erected in 1866, though no one really knows why. He only ever visited this area once, on a shooting weekend (bagging more beaters than grouse), so it is unlikely the citizens of Baslow erected it to commemorate this. More likely it is just a partner for Nelson's Monument, erected in 1810 on Birchen's Edge in merciful thanks that this one-armed, one-eyed Admiral never came here to shoot at all.

Our way now lies westward to Baslow along the wide sandy track descending to the village outskirts where it becomes a metalled road which, if followed straight, brings you out on the A623 opposite the church. After dragging yourself out of the Prince of Wales (see pub guide) walk through the churchyard to the bridge. Note the unusual clock face which has 'Victoria 1897' in place of numerals, a commemoration to the Queen's Diamond Jubilee. Two interesting objects are on display in a glass case just inside the church: one is the pitch pipe used to tune the organ when it was installed in 1856; the other is a dog whip used for "whipping ye dogges forthe of ye churche in tyme of divyne service."

Tell your companion to get a move on as it is already V past A. As you leave note the small guardhouse on the bridge which was probably a toll booth where merchants would be charged a fixed sum to enter Baslow prior to trading. It is on record that in 1500 you could be fined 6s 8d for illegally transporting millstones across the bridge.

The author at Wellington's Monument. Stage 7

Over the bridge bear left, then left again and right at the roundabout. Pass the sports ground and about 100 yards before the Cavendish Hotel you will find some steps leading down to a path. This crosses a stream before joining the track which you follow to the right into Chatsworth. You enter the park through a large metal kissing gate and immediately it is like entering a different world. It is as though you had stepped back in time to when there were no fields bounded by stone walls and barbed wire, only the open miles of verdant rolling pasture, natural woodland and swirling river.

The first notable building to come into view is the Hunting Tower, which stands on the top of the thickly wooded slope over on your left. The ladies would gather here supposedly to watch their menfolk hunt. More likely they had a good old chinwag. Passing the nursery you catch your first glimpse of the house through the trees, then beyond the cricket ground the path runs beside the Derwent to Queen Mary's Bower, which is surrounded by a dry moat.

The bower is the oldest surviving building on the estate, a summer retreat built at the same time as the original house, of which nothing now remains. The owners were Sir William Cavendish and his wife Elizabeth Hardwick; and it is around Bess, as she is better known, that the early history of Chatsworth revolves.

Bess was a shrewd woman. She outlived several husbands, each one richer than the last, and all of them carefully chosen because they were either weak, old or ailing. In 1570 her fourth husband, George

Queen Mary's Bower, Chatsworth

Queen Mary's Bower, Chatsworth 77

*Unusual clock face
Baslow Church*

Talbot, the gout-ridden sixth Earl of Shrewsbury, was made guardian to Mary Queen of Scots, who was a frequent visitor to Chatsworth during her exile. Mary spent most of her time at the bower, probably to keep out of Bess' way, and until recently her coat of arms could be seen above the entrance.

These were troubled times for Bess, for not only did she suspect that Old George's devotion to Mary went beyond that of guardian, she herself was imprisoned in the Tower of London for a time because Elizabeth I suspected her of conniving on Mary's behalf. Bess was so angry she could not wait for George to snuff it, she left him and returned to her birthplace at Hardwick Hall, near Chesterfield. After George Talbot died Chatsworth again became a seat of the Cavendish family as the estate passed in succession to two of Bess' sons by her marriage to Sir William. It has remained in this family ever since.

The house as you see it today was built between 1686 and 1707 by the first Duke of Devonshire, a title of no relevance whatsoever (the name must have been drawn out of a hat, or perhaps the scribe had had one too many and got his counties mixed up!). No further significant alterations were made until the mid-eighteenth century when the fourth duke employed Capability Brown to landscape the park. The stables and elegant bridge, which you now cross, were also built around this time. The present day gardens were laid out by the sixth duke in the nineteenth century, employing another famous gardener, Joseph Paxton, the guy who built Crystal Palace (the original glass one, not the football team).

Ascend the path on the right leading to the estate village called Edensor (pronounced Ensor). The church, built on the site of an older one in 1867, houses an elaborate monument to the two sons of Bess of Hardwick and also displays in the choir vestry a wreath sent by Queen Victoria for the funeral of Lord Frederick Cavendish. Among the monuments in the churchyard is a small stone commemorating the visit of President John F Kennedy to the grave of his sister in 1963.

Walk up the road with the church on your left, then climb the steps at the footpath sign to Rowsley. Once through the gate aim slightly right across the pasture, following waymarks past the end of a strip of fenced conifers en-route to the wood at the top of the hill. Here you will find a notice board beside a gate (viewpoint). It is in this part of the park that fallow deer graze, so walk silently and keep an eye out for the herd. These graceful animals are a sight to behold, especially in surroundings like this. They are timid and easily startled, but with caution it should be possible to get close enough for a photo.

Once over the stile follow the track through the wood and out the other side to a signpost at a crosstracks. Before taking the right fork look over to your left at the odd, but attractive, cottage. It was built by the sixth duke in the Russian style to make the Czar feel at home during a visit which never actually materialised.

Walk straight up the middle of two long fields to a pond in the far left-hand corner of the pasture. Cross the stiles, pass just to the left of the trees and head down the hill, pausing perhaps, if this is your last day, for a moment of poignant reflection as Bakewell comes into view. Locate the ladder-stile and descend steeply through the wood.

When you meet a track either turn left and then sharp right, or officially right and immediately left to continue by the stream. This is the waymarked right of way but is the steeper and stonier of the two paths. Both paths unite lower down before emerging out of the wood to cross the golf course. Duck immediately if you hear a shout of 'Fore!' The members at Bakewell never miss an opportunity to bag a stray pheasant with a low four iron off the tee. Cross the bridge over the disused railway and continue down the field edge to join a track leading out onto the road. Cross over and enter the showground, turning right at the office for the town centre.

Anti-clockwise Directions   Bakewell to Hathersage

Follow the guidebook into the showground. When you reach the Agricultural Society office turn left. Cross the road and ascend the farm track which follows the wall on your right. Cross the disused railway, staying with the track as it swings left across the golf course and into the woods. Take the left fork at the stream and ascend steeply with the stream to a ladder-stile leading into Calton Pastures. Aim half-right up the slope, passing through the isolated copse to the stile next to the pond. Cross the next stile then walk down the middle of two long fields. Turn left at the crosstracks, pass through the wood - pause to admire the superb view over Chatsworth - then continue down the slope towards Edensor church. The stile is just to the left, next to an electricity sub-station.

Turn right into the estate village, cross the main road and follow the path to Chatsworth House. Cross the bridge and turn left past Queen Mary's Bower, following the river to Baslow.

Walk up School Lane and the track beyond to Wellington's Monument. Pass the Eagle Stone, cross the road at Curbar Gap and follow the path along the edge of the escarpment to the B6054. Cross over to the gate on the left, a few yards down the road. Cross the dip and keep left below the car park to a stile. After about 200 yards, when the descending path levels out, look for the well defined path forking left. Follow this down through Hay Wood and turn right along a farm track to the road.

Cross over to the stile at the far side of the garage and follow the

Toll Booth, Baslow

riverside path to Leadmill Bridge. Cross the main road and follow the fieldpath opposite and the lane beyond into Hathersage. Turn left at the George Hotel for the hostel.

Wherever you started from I hope the weather was kind and that you thoroughly enjoyed your holiday. (No blisters, I trust?) If you would like to write and tell me about your walk, especially any changes you may have encountered, I would love to hear from you. And if you can spare a photograph of yourself or your group for my White Peak Way scrapbook, so much the better. Please enclose a SAE if you would like me to reply. My address is: 87 Ling Road, Chesterfield, Derbyshire, S40 3HU.

APPENDIX I: THE COUNTRY CODE

To the best of my knowledge the White Peak Way is entirely along existing rights of way or across land to which the public has access. Even so the land is still privately owned, be it by the National Trust or the hardworking farmer, and therefore it is imperative that you understand and obey the Country Code.

>Enjoy the countryside and respect its life and work.
>
>Guard against all risk of fire.
>
>Fasten all gates.
>
>Keep dogs under close control.
>
>Keep to public paths across farmland.
>
>Use gates and stiles to cross fences, hedges and walls.
>
>Leave crops, livestock and machinery alone.
>
>Take your litter with you.
>
>Do not pollute water.
>
>Protect wildlife, plants and trees.
>
>Take special care on country roads.
>
>Make no unnecessary noise.

And remember, if you do stray off course, a little respect and courtesy will usually win over an irate landowner.

APPENDIX II: YOUTH HOSTEL INFORMATION

YHA Northern Region operate a Booking Bureau for the White Peak Way, which is an easy and convenient way to book your accommodation for the entire week in one go, and with the guarantee of a bed every night. All the hostels serve breakfast and evening meals, and these may also be booked in advance. YHA members should refer to the current handbook for details of opening times, closed nights and overnight charges. All enquiries regarding the White Peak Way should be addressed to:

YHA Northern Region
PO Box 11
Matlock
Derbyshire
DE4 2XA
Tel: 01629 939215 (calls at local rate 24 hours)
Fax: 01629 824571

At the moment YHA also run inclusive one-week guided walking holidays on the WPW with luggage transfer included. For details of price and availability contact the address above.

The Hostels

Bakewell 01629 812313
A modern 36 bed hostel perched on a hill overlooking the town, and only a few minutes walk from the centre.

Youlgreave 01629 636518
This 46 bed hostel of great character is housed in the former Co-op. Has always been renowned for the quality of the food.

Elton 01629 650394
A simple hostel of 32 beds with a limited breakfast and evening snack menu. Can be used as an alternative to Youlgreave to shorten the distance to Ilam, but not featured in the Booking Bureau.

Ilam Hall 01335 350212
An impressive National Trust mansion, set in beautiful parkland on the banks of the Manifold. Has every convenience including family accommodation. 148 beds.

Hartington Hall 01298 84223
Another magnificent building, a manor house from the seventeenth century. Also offers family accommodation. 120 beds

Ravenstor 01298 871826
Another impressive country house owned by the National Trust, set in spacious wooded grounds high above the River Wye. Was voted all-round favourite hostel by charity walkers in 1991. 84 beds.

Buxton 01298 22287
55 beds in a large house on the outskirts of town, occasionally used by the Booking Bureau as an alternative when Ravenstor is fully booked.

Castleton 01433 620235
The most recently refurbished of the WPW hostels, situated in a fifteenth century hall and vicarage, where family accommodation is now available. 150 beds.

Hathersage 01433 650493
Mike Rosser, the warden at Hathersage, founded the Booking Bureau in 1986 and still runs it from his office at this cosy 42 bed hostel. Hathersage is a popular starting point for the walk, as it can be reached by rail.

APPENDIX III: PUB GUIDE

Ale quaffing is a popular pastime. On a walking holiday in rural areas it is the only pastime. But at least you can indulge with a clear conscience if not a clear head, and you needn't worry about the calories or the breathalyser.

Principally, though, the pub is a place to relax at the end of a hard day on the trail, or in the middle of the day whilst still on the trail, or even at the end of the trail before the end of a hard day on the trail, by which time you are past caring about the damn trail! It is also a good place to meet fellow alcoholics (sorry, walkers) on the same jaunt as yourselves. If not, there is always the beer!

The Peak District is good drinking country with a flourishing free trade and a wide choice of brews, most of them real ales. For the earlier editions of this guide, I traipsed round every pub on the walk sampling everything on offer, under protest, of course, and only for the benefit of my readers, only to discover that within six months the guide was completely out of date. So in this edition there are no personal recommendations or details of what beers are available. Suffice it to say, it is possible to get a drink and food every lunchtime and evening on the main route, and in some places there is a choice. A high percentage of White Peak Wayfarers plan their entire holiday using this section of the book alone! I can't think why!

Stage 1
Bakewell has a wealth of pubs, most of them residential hotels. The Queen's Arms Hotel and the Wheatsheaf are in the 1996 Good Beer Guide. Evening meals are no problem.

The Druid Inn at Birchover lies directly on the route and is noted for its food. There is a spacious patio for outside drinkers and diners.

The Bull's Head in Youlgreave is a Good Beer Guide pub with a varied menu and reasonably priced accommodation. Youlgreave also has a chippy virtually next door to the hostel. When it's open the smell is irresistible.

Stage 2

The Waterloo Inn at Biggin is a convenient lunchtime halt. It is a splendidly situated pub with a large lawn containing picnic tables. Food is served and there is even a campsite attached.

Anyone overnighting in Alstonefield has the George, a superb village inn, noted for quality ale and food. Those staying at Ilam have to walk back to the Izaak Walton Hotel in Dovedale. On your way past note the stile leading onto the premises, as the fieldpath is the shortest route from Ilam Hall. You walk round the front to the other side for the entrance to the bar.

Stage 3

Ye Olde Royal Oak in Wetton is popular lunchtimes and evenings, depending on your itinerary. It is an ideal overnight stop for backpackers as it has both a campsite and camping barn. There is usually a wide choice of real ales and food, lunchtime and evening.

Hartington has two pubs close to one another, the Devonshire and the Charles Cotton. I'd try the Charles Cotton first.

Stage 4

If you mourn the passing of the traditional English country pub, you really must visit the Quiet Woman at Earl Sterndale. It is an unspoilt gem, and has never once been omitted from the Good Beer Guide. Snacks only.

Hostellers at Ravenstor pass the Angler's Rest at Millers Dale (grid ref. 143733) on the way through. To return, though, it is quicker to walk down the main road. You may need a torch.

Tideswell has several pubs, both the George and Horse & Jockey are Good Beer Guide, and both serve food. If you are camping or staying in Blackwell, you have a road walk of exactly one mile to the Waterloo, situated on the A6 (grid ref. 133714).

Stage 5

The Devonshire at Peak Forest is a convenient lunchtime halt, popular with walkers. In Castleton you are spoiled for choice, with six or seven to choose from. The Bull's Head is a regular in the Good Beer

Guide, has a pool room and plenty of space to stretch weary limbs. The two just down from the hostel are also worth a visit. There is also a chippy just behind the hostel.

Stage 6

After descending Lose Hill and prior to climbing Win Hill you could walk a quarter mile down the road towards Hope for the Cheshire Cheese, an extremely popular ramblers pub, serving good food.

Hathersage has a good choice. The Scotsman's Pack is handy following a visit to the church (see text). It is residential, in the Good Beer Guide and serves evening meals. The Little John and the Hathersage Inn are close to the youth hostel.

Stage 7

The Grouse Inn (grid ref. 258779) is only a short walk off the route, reachable by fieldpath from the car park at 256778, but may come a little too early for lunch. Baslow may be more suitable, and there is plenty of choice, the Prince of Wales being the nearest.

The White Peak Way was conceived, researched and written at a time when the author worked at a maternity hospital. Sticking with medicine, in 1989 and 1991, WPW charity walkers raised over £33,000 for the Heart Transplant Unit at Sheffield's Northern General Hospital, where the author is currently employed, despite cuts in the Health Service. This money was used to buy a flat near the hospital for the convenience of patients and relatives, many of whom live a fair distance from Sheffield. Mr Haslam is an uneducated and rather boring individual who does his utmost to avoid doing interesting things.

APPENDIX IV: INFORMATION TABLE

| | Accommodation | | | | | | Facilities | | | | | |
	Hotel	Inn	Guest House	Youth Hostel	Campsite	Camping Barn	Shop	Pub	Post Office	Pharmacy	Tea Shop	Bank
Bakewell	√	√	√	√		√	√	√	√	√	√	√
Rowsley	√	√	√				√	√	√			
Stanton in Peak			√				√	√	√			
Birchover					√	√	√	√				
* Elton			√	√				√			√	
Youlgreave		√	√	√	√		√	√	√			
Biggin	√		√		√			√				
Milldale								√			√	
* Alstonefield			√				√	√	√		√	
* Thorpe	√		√					√				
Dovedale	√							√				
Ilam				√	√						√	
* Wettonmill											√	
Wetton		√	√		√	√		√				
Hartington	√		√	√	√		√	√	√		√	
Earl Sterndale			√					√				
* Blackwell			√		√							
Millers Dale			√					√			√	
Ravenstor				√								
* Buxton	√	√	√	√			√	√	√	√	√	√
Tideswell			√				√	√	√	√	√	√
Peak Forest		√	√				√	√	√			
Castleton		√	√	√	√	√	√	√	√		√	
* Hope								√				
Shatton											√	
Hathersage	√	√	√	√	√		√	√	√	√	√	√
Baslow	√	√	√				√	√			√	
Edensor											√	
* Off main route												

NOTES ON THE WAY

CICERONE GUIDES

Cicerone publish a wide range of reliable guides to walking and climbing in Britain, and other general interest books.

LAKE DISTRICT - General Books

CONISTON COPPER A History
CHRONICLES OF MILNTHORPE
A DREAM OF EDEN -LAKELAND DALES
EDEN TAPESTRY
THE HIGH FELLS OF LAKELAND
KENDAL A SOCIAL HISTORY
LAKELAND - A taste to remember (Recipes)
LAKELAND VILLAGES
LAKELAND TOWNS
LAKELAND PANORAMAS
THE LAKERS
THE LOST RESORT? (Morecambe)
LOST LANCASHIRE (Furness area)
REFLECTIONS ON THE LAKES
AN ILLUSTRATED COMPANION INTO LAKELAND

LAKE DISTRICT - Guide Books

THE BORDERS OF LAKELAND
BIRDS OF MORECAMBE BAY
CASTLES IN CUMBRIA
CONISTON COPPER MINES Field Guide
THE CUMBRIA CYCLE WAY
THE CUMBRIA WAY & ALLERDALE RAMBLE
THE EDEN WAY
IN SEARCH OF WESTMORLAND
SHORT WALKS IN LAKELAND-1: SOUTH LAKELAND
SHORT WALKS IN LAKELAND- 2:NORTH LAKELAND
SCRAMBLES IN THE LAKE DISTRICT
MORE SCRAMBLES IN THE LAKE DISTRICT
THE TARNS OF LAKELAND VOL 1 - WEST
THE TARNS OF LAKELAND VOL 2 - EAST
WALKING ROUND THE LAKES
WALKS IN SILVERDALE/ARNSIDE
WESTMORLAND HERITAGE WALK
WINTER CLIMBS IN THE LAKE DISTRICT

NORTHERN ENGLAND (outside the Lakes

BIRDWATCHING ON MERSEYSIDE
CANAL WALKS Vol 1 North
CANOEISTS GUIDE TO THE NORTH EAST
THE CLEVELAND WAY & MISSING LINK
THE DALES WAY

DOUGLAS VALLEY WAY
FAMILY WALKS IN BOWLAND
WALKING IN THE FOREST OF BOWLAND
HADRIANS WALL Vol 1 The Wall Walk
HADRIANS WALL VOL 2 Walks around the Wall
HERITAGE TRAILS IN NW ENGLAND
THE ISLE OF MAN COASTAL PATH
IVORY TOWERS & DRESSED STONES (Follies)
THE LANCASTER CANAL
LANCASTER CANAL WALKS
A WALKERS GUIDE TO THE LANCASTER CANAL
WALKS FROM THE LEEDS-LIVERPOOL CANAL
LAUGHS ALONG THE PENNINE WAY
A NORTHERN COAST-TO-COAST
NORTH YORK MOORS Walks
ON THE RUFFSTUFF 84 Bike rides in Northern England
THE REIVERS WAY (Northumberland)
THE RIBBLE WAY
THE TEESDALE WAY
WALKING IN COUNTY DURHAM
WALKING IN LANCASHIRE
WALKING DOWN THE LUNE
WALKING IN THE SOUTH PENNINES
WALKING IN THE NORTH PENNINES
WALKING IN THE WOLDS
WALKS IN THE YORKSHIRE DALES (3 VOL)
WALKS IN LANCASHIRE WITCH COUNTRY
WALKS IN THE NORTH YORK MOORS (2 VOL)
WALKS TO YORKSHIRE WATERFALLS (2 vol)
WATERFALL WALKS -TEESDALE & THE HIGH PENNINES
WALKS ON THE WEST PENNINE MOORS
WALKING NORTHERN RAILWAYS (2 vol)
THE YORKSHIRE DALES A walker's guide

DERBYSHIRE PEAK DISTRICT & EAST MIDLANDS

KINDER LOG
HIGH PEAK WALKS
WHITE PEAK WAY
WHITE PEAK WALKS - 2 Vols
WEEKEND WALKS IN THE PEAK DISTRICT
THE VIKING WAY
THE DEVIL'S MILL / WHISTLING CLOUGH (Novels)

Other guides are constantly being added to the Cicerone List.
Available from bookshops, outdoor equipment shops or direct (send s.a.e. for price list) from
CICERONE, 2 POLICE SQUARE, MILNTHORPE, CUMBRIA, LA7 7PY

CICERONE GUIDES
Cicerone publish a wide range of reliable guides to walking and climbing in Britain, and other general interest books.

WALES, WELSH BORDER & WEST MIDLANDS
ASCENT OF SNOWDON
THE BRECON BEACONS
WALKING IN CHESHIRE
THE CHESHIRE CYCLE WAY
CLWYD ROCK
HEREFORD & THE WYE VALLEY A Walker's Guide
HILLWALKING IN SNOWDONIA
HILL WALKING IN WALES (2 Vols)
THE LLEYN PENINSULA COASTAL PATH
THE MOUNTAINS OF ENGLAND & WALES Vol 1 WALES
WALKING OFFA'S DYKE PATH
THE RIDGES OF SNOWDONIA
ROCK CLIMBS IN WEST MIDLANDS
SARN HELEN Walking Roman Road
SCRAMBLES IN SNOWDONIA
SEVERN WALKS
THE SHROPSHIRE HILLS A Walker's Guide
SNOWDONIA WHITE WATER SEA & SURF
WALKING DOWN THE WYE
A WELSH COAST TO COAST WALK
WELSH WINTER CLIMBS

SOUTH & SOUTH WEST ENGLAND
WALKING IN CORNWALL
WALKING IN THE CHILTERNS
COTSWOLD WAY
COTSWOLD WALKS (3 VOLS)
WALKING ON DARTMOOR
WALKERS GUIDE TO DARTMOOR PUBS
WALKING IN DEVON
WALKING IN DORSET
EXMOOR & THE QUANTOCKS
THE GRAND UNION CANAL WALK
THE KENNET & AVON WALK
LONDON THEME WALKS
WALKING IN OXFORDSHIRE
AN OXBRIDGE WALK
A SOUTHERN COUNTIES BIKE GUIDE
THE SOUTHERN-COAST-TO-COAST

SOUTH DOWNS WAY & DOWNS LINK
SOUTH WEST WAY - 2 Vol
THE TWO MOORS WAY Dartmoor-Exmoor
WALKS IN KENT Bk 2
THE WEALDWAY & VANGUARD WAY

SCOTLAND
THE BORDER COUNTRY - WALKERS GUIDE
BORDER PUBS & INNS A Walker's Guide
CAIRNGORMS WINTER CLIMBS
WALKING THE GALLOWAY HILLS
THE ISLAND OF RHUM
THE ISLE OF SKYE - A Walker's Guide
THE SCOTTISH GLENS (Mountainbike Guide)
  Book 1:THE CAIRNGORM GLENS
  Book 2 THE ATHOLL GLENS
  Book 3 THE GLENS OF RANNOCH
  Book 4 THE GLENS OF TROSSACH
  Book 5 THE GLENS OF ARGYLL
  Book 6 THE GREAT GLEN
SCOTTISH RAILWAY WALKS
SCRAMBLES IN LOCHABER
SCRAMBLES IN SKYE
SKI TOURING IN SCOTLAND
TORRIDON A Walker's Guide
WALKS from the WEST HIGHLAND RAILWAY
WINTER CLIMBS BEN NEVIS & GLENCOE

REGIONAL BOOKS UK & IRELAND
THE ALTERNATIVE PENNINE WAY
THE ALTERNATIVE COAST TO COAST
LANDS END TO JOHN O'GROATS CYCLE GUIDE
CANAL WALKS Vol.1: North
CANAL WALKS Vol.2: Midlands
CANAL WALKS Vol.3: South
LIMESTONE - 100 BEST CLIMBS
THE PACKHORSE BRIDGES OF ENGLAND
THE RELATIVE HILLS OF BRITAIN
THE MOUNTAINS OF ENGLAND & WALES
  VOL 1 WALES, VOL 2 ENGLAND
THE MOUNTAINS OF IRELAND
THE IRISH COAST TO COAST WALK

Also a full range of EUROPEAN and OVERSEAS guidebooks - walking, long distance trails, scrambling, ice-climbing, rock climbing.

Other guides are constantly being added to the Cicerone List.
Available from bookshops, outdoor equipment shops or direct (send s.a.e. for price list) from
CICERONE, 2 POLICE SQUARE, MILNTHORPE, CUMBRIA, LA7 7PY

CICERONE GUIDES

Cicerone publish a wide range of reliable guides to walking and climbing worldwide

FRANCE, BELGIUM & LUXEMBOURG

THE BRITTANY COASTAL PATH
CHAMONIX MONT BLANC - A Walking Guide
THE CORSICAN HIGH LEVEL ROUTE: GR20
FRENCH ROCK
THE PYRENEAN TRAIL: GR10
THE RLS (Stevenson) TRAIL
ROCK CLIMBS IN BELGIUM & LUXEMBOURG
ROCK CLIMBS IN THE VERDON
TOUR OF MONT BLANC
TOUR OF THE OISANS: GR54
TOUR OF THE QUEYRAS
TOUR OF THE VANOISE
WALKING IN THE ARDENNES
WALKING THE FRENCH ALPS: GR5
WALKING IN HAUTE SAVOIE
WALKING IN THE TARENTAISE & BEAUFORTAIN ALPS
WALKING THE FRENCH GORGES (Provence)
WALKS IN VOLCANO COUNTRY (Auvergne)
THE WAY OF ST JAMES: GR65

FRANCE / SPAIN

WALKS AND CLIMBS IN THE PYRENEES
ROCK CLIMBS IN THE PYRENEES

SPAIN & PORTUGAL

WALKING IN THE ALGARVE
ANDALUSIAN ROCK CLIMBS
BIRDWATCHING IN MALLORCA
COSTA BLANCA CLIMBS
MOUNTAIN WALKS ON THE COSTA BLANCA
ROCK CLIMBS IN MAJORCA, IBIZA & TENERIFE
WALKING IN MALLORCA
THE MOUNTAINS OF CENTRAL SPAIN
THROUGH THE SPANISH PYRENEES: GR11

WALKING IN THE SIERRA NEVADA
WALKS & CLIMBS IN THE PICOS DE EUROPA
THE WAY OF ST JAMES: SPAIN

SWITZERLAND including adjacent parts of France and Italy

THE ALPINE PASS ROUTE
THE BERNESE ALPS
CENTRAL SWITZERLAND
CHAMONIX TO ZERMATT The Walker's Haute Route
THE GRAND TOUR OF MONTE ROSA (inc Italy) 2 vols
WALKS IN THE ENGADINE
THE JURA - Walking the High Route and Winter Ski Traverses
WALKING IN TICINO
THE VALAIS - A Walking Guide

GERMANY / AUSTRIA / EASTERN & NORTHERN EUROPE

WALKING IN THE BAVARIAN ALPS
GERMANY'S ROMANTIC ROAD A guide for walkers and cyclists
HUT-TO-HUT IN THE STUBAI ALPS
THE HIGH TATRAS
KING LUDWIG WAY
KLETTERSTEIG - Scrambles
MOUNTAIN WALKING IN AUSTRIA
WALKING IN THE BLACK FOREST
WALKING IN THE HARZ MOUNTAINS
WALKING IN NORWAY
WALKING IN THE SALZKAMMERGUT

CICERONE GUIDES

Cicerone publish a wide range of reliable guides to walking and climbing worldwide

ITALY & SLOVENIA

ALTA VIA - High Level Walks in the Dolomites
THE CENTRAL APENNINES OF ITALY Walks, scrambles & Climbs
THE GRAND TOUR OF MONTE ROSA (inc Switzerland)
WALKS IN ITALY'S GRAN PARADISO
LONG DISTANCE WALKS IN THE GRAN PARADISO
ITALIAN ROCK - Rock Climbs in Northern Italy
VIA FERRATA - Scrambles in the Dolomites
WALKING IN THE DOLOMITES
WALKS IN THE JULIAN ALPS

MEDITERRANEAN COUNTRIES

THE ATLAS MOUNTAINS
CRETE: Off the beaten track
WALKING IN CYPRUS
THE MOUNTAINS OF GREECE
THE MOUNTAINS OF TURKEY
TREKS & CLIMBS IN WADI RUM, JORDAN
THE ALA DAG - Climbs & Treks (Turkey)

HIMALAYA & OTHER COUNTRIES

ANNAPURNA TREKKERS GUIDE
EVEREST - A TREKKER'S GUIDE
LANGTANG, GOSAINKUND & HELAMBU A Trekker's Guide
MOUNTAIN WALKING IN AFRICA 1: KENYA
ROCK CLIMBS IN HONG KONG
TREKKING IN THE CAUCAUSUS
ADVENTURE TREKS IN NEPAL
ADVENTURE TREKS - WESTERN NORTH AMERICA
CLASSIC TRAMPS IN NEW ZEALAND

GENERAL OUTDOOR BOOKS

THE ADVENTURE ALTERNATIVE
ENCYCLOPAEDIA OF MOUNTAINEERING
FAMILY CAMPING
FAR HORIZONS - Adventure Travel for All!
THE TREKKER'S HANDBOOK
FIRST AID FOR HILLWALKERS
THE HILLWALKERS MANUAL
LIMESTONE -100 BEST CLIMBS IN BRITAIN
MOUNTAIN WEATHER
SNOW & ICE TECHNIQUES
ROPE TECHNIQUES IN MOUNTAINEERING

CANOEING

CANOEIST'S GUIDE TO THE NORTH EAST
SNOWDONIA WILD WATER, SEA & SURF
WILDWATER CANOEING

CARTOON BOOKS IDEAL GIFTS

ON FOOT & FINGER
ON MORE FEET & FINGERS
LAUGHS ALONG THE PENNINE WAY
THE WALKERS

A full range of guidebooks to walking - short walks, family walks, long distance treks, scrambling, ice-climbing, rock climbing, and other adventurous pursuits worldwide

---

*Other guides are constantly being added to the Cicerone List.
Available from bookshops, outdoor equipment shops or direct (send for price list)
from CICERONE, 2 POLICE SQUARE, MILNTHORPE, CUMBRIA, LA7 7PY*

White Peak Way

yha *Accommodation Booking Services for independent walkers*

The easy and convenient way to plan your walk. Let us book your YHA accommodation for you along the route. You tell us the dates - we do the rest. All ages welcome!!

- ◆ *Comfortable Youth Hostels directly on the route.*
- ◆ *Dinner, bed & breakfast & packed lunches available. Plus self-catering facilities. You choose to meet your budget.*
- ◆ *Comfortable bunk-bedded rooms and lounges plus drying facilities for wet clothing and boots.*
- ◆ *Low administration costs. We charge just £3.00 per person to organise your holiday.*

YHA - Welcoming walkers for over 60 years
Tel: 01629 825850 (24 hours.)

Printed by CARNMOR PRINT & DESIGN
95-97 LONDON ROAD, PRESTON, LANCASHIRE, UK.